What Is a Globe?

Monday

1. A globe is a model of _________________________

2. A globe and Earth are shaped like a _____________________________ .

Tuesday

1. Name the imaginary line shown on the globes.

   ____

2. Name two continents.

   ____

   ____

Wednesday

1. What is the most northern point on Earth called?

   ____

2. What is the most southern point on Earth called?

   ____

What Is a Globe?

Thursday

1. Is Australia south or north of the equator?

____

2. Is most of South America north or south of the equator?

____

Friday

1. On which continent do you live?

____

2. Do you live north or south of the equator?

____

Challenge

On all three globes, color the oceans blue.
Color the continents green.

What Is a Map?

Monday

1. What is a map?

   ____

   ____

2. What does this map show?

   ____

Tuesday

1. How many continents does this map show? _______________

2. Write the names of three continents.

   ____

   ____

Wednesday

1. How many oceans are on this map? _______________

2. Write the names of the oceans.

   ____

   ____

What Is a Map?

Thursday

1. Which continents border the Atlantic Ocean?

____

____

2. Which two continents do <u>not</u> touch any other continent?

____

Friday

1. On which continent do you live?

____

2. Which continent is your closest neighbor?

____

Challenge

- Color the oceans blue.
- Color North America yellow.
- Color South America red.
- Color Antarctica gray.
- Color Africa purple.
- Color Europe orange.
- Color Asia green.
- Color Australia brown.

Parts of a Map

Monday

1. What is the title of the map?

2. What is a map key?

Tuesday

1. Write the names of three symbols used in the map key.

2. Name the symbol used for Lupe's Taco Shack.

Wednesday

1. What does a compass rose show?

2. Which directions are shown on this compass rose?

Parts of a Map

Thursday

1. How many avenues are on this map? What are their names?

2. Does Highway 68 run east and west, or north and south?

Friday

1. Is Night's Inn on the west or east end of Beach Road?

2. Which two businesses are east of Second Avenue?

Challenge

What would you call this small town? Write a new title for this map.
Write the new title on the map.

Intermediate Directions

Monday

1. What are the intermediate directions on the compass rose?

2. Write the letters used for the four intermediate directions.

Tuesday

1. Which building is east of the library?

2. Which building is southwest of the school?

Wednesday

1. Start at the post office. In which direction is the police station?

2. Start at the library. In which direction is the school?

Intermediate Directions

Thursday

1. Which building is northwest of the post office?

   ____

2. Does First Avenue run east and west or north and south?

   ____

Friday

1. Start at the west end of Main Street. In which direction is the fountain?

   ____

2. What is found where Main Street and First Avenue cross?

   ____

Challenge

On the map, draw a book in the southeast corner of the library.
Draw a flagpole in the southwest corner of the school.

A Map Grid

Monday

1. In which square would you find the park entrance?

   ____

2. In which square would you go to play basketball?

   ____

Tuesday

1. In which square can you get a drink of water?

   ____

2. In which square can you rest on a park bench?

   ____

Wednesday

1. How many squares does the picnic area include?

   ____

2. Name the squares for the picnic area.

   ____

A Map Grid

Thursday

1. How many squares does the baseball diamond include?

   ____

2. Name the squares for the baseball area.

   ____

Friday

1. What is above square E5?

   ____

2. The playground equipment is in which four squares?

   ____

Challenge

Find square C2. Draw a picture in this square of something you might see in a park.

A Map Grid and a Map Index

Monday

1. Which numbers are on this map grid?

____

2. Which letters are on the map grid?

____

Tuesday

1. Which city is in square B4?

____

2. Which city is in square C2?

____

Wednesday

1. In which square are the cities of Birmingham and Hoover?

____

2. In which square is the city of Mobile?

____

A Map Grid and a Map Index

Thursday

1. Huntsville shares a square with which other city?

   ____

2. In which square is Decatur?

   ____

Friday

1. What is the capital of Alabama? In which two squares is it?

   ____

2. What does the map index show?

   ____

   ____

Challenge

On the map:

- Color square E2 red.
- Color square G4 green.

A Map Key

Monday

1. What is the name of the capital city?

____

2. What is the name of the large city shown on the map?

____

Tuesday

1. Write the name of each medium-size city.

____

____

2. Write the name of each small town.

____

Wednesday

1. Write the names of the two rivers that are borders.

____

2. Write the names of the two rivers that are <u>not</u> borders.

____

A Map Key

Thursday

1. Write the name of the medium-size city that is close to the Wisconsin border.

   ____

2. Write the name of the lake that shares a border with Illinois.

   ____

Friday

1. Write the name of the large city that shares a border with Lake Michigan.

   ____

2. Write the name of the border state that is east of Decatur and Aurora.

   ____

Challenge

On the map, write the names of the states that border Illinois.

A Map Scale

Monday

1. How many cities are shown on this map?

   ____

2. What is the capital of Texas?

   ____

Tuesday

1. Texas is the _________________ largest state in the United States.

2. Is Amarillo in northern or southern Texas?

   ____

Wednesday

1. On the map scale, ½ inch = _________ miles.

2. On the map scale, 1 inch = _________ miles.

A Map Scale

Thursday

1. Is El Paso in eastern or western Texas?

____

2. Which city shown on the map is the farthest south?

____

Friday

1. On the map, El Paso is about __________ inches from Abilene.

2. About how many miles is El Paso from Abilene?

____

Challenge

Measure the distance in inches between Houston and Brownsville. Use the scale to find about how many miles that represents. Write your answer on the map page.

Daily Geography Practice • EMC 6853 • © Evan-Moor Corporation

Picturing the United States

Monday

1. Does the eastern or western half of the U.S. have larger states?

2. Where are most of the smallest states found?

Tuesday

1. Name two states that border the Pacific Ocean.

2. Which ocean borders the states that are located in the east?

Wednesday

1. How many states border the Gulf of Mexico?

2. Which two states are <u>not</u> attached to the rest of the country?

Picturing the United States

Thursday

1. Which country and which oceans border Alaska?

   ____

2. Are the Hawaiian Islands north, south, east, or west of Alaska?

   ____

Friday

1. Is Canada north or south of the United States?

   ____

2. Is Mexico north or south of the United States?

   ____

Challenge

Close your eyes and picture the map of the United States. On a piece of blank paper, draw a map of the outline shape of the United States. Look at the real map to see how you did.

Picturing North America

Monday

1. Which continent is shown on the map?

____

2. Name the three largest countries on the continent.

____

____

Tuesday

1. Which large country is north of the United States?

____

2. Which large country is south of the United States?

____

Wednesday

1. Which large country has lots of islands to the north?

____

2. Which U.S. state borders Canada and <u>not</u> the U.S.?

____

Picturing North America

Thursday

1. How many oceans border North America? Name them.

   ____

   ____

2. Name the two countries that border southern Mexico.

   ____

Friday

1. Name the largest island country east of Mexico.

   ____

2. Name the continent that is south of North America.

   ____

Challenge

On the map, trace the outline shape of North America in dark red. Place a blank piece of paper over the map. Trace over the lines that show through onto the blank piece of paper. Look at your drawing of North America. Close your eyes and make a mental picture of the shape of North America.

Transportation Routes in a Town

Monday

1. Name three kinds of routes that are shown on the map.

   ____

   ____

2. Which highway leads to the airport? ______________________

Tuesday

1. On which street is the train station?

   ____

2. Does the bike path go around the lake, the school, or the shopping center?

   ____

Wednesday

1. Which two routes are near the lake?

   ____

2. On which street is the entrance to the police station?

   ____

Transportation Routes in a Town

Thursday

1. In which direction do the train tracks run?

2. Which streets cross the train tracks?

Friday

1. Which street do you cross to get from the school to the park?

2. Which route runs alongside the railroad tracks?

Challenge

Use a blue marker to highlight the bike path on the map.

A Road Map: South Dakota

Monday

1. Name the interstate highways shown on the map.

2. Name the U.S. highways shown on the map.

Tuesday

1. In which direction does Interstate Highway 29 run?

2. Which U.S. highway runs through the capital city of Pierre?

Wednesday

1. In which direction does Interstate Highway 90 run?

2. Which U.S. highway runs through Mobridge?

A Road Map: South Dakota

Thursday

1. Which interstate highway runs through the city of Mitchell?

   ____

2. Name the cities along Interstate 29.

   ____

Friday

1. Which U.S. highways intersect in the city of Aberdeen?

   ____

2. Which interstate highway joins U.S. Highway 14?

   ____

Challenge

- Highlight the routes of the interstate highways in yellow.
- Highlight the routes of the U.S. highways in orange.

Waterways of the United States

Monday

1. Which four kinds of waterways are shown on the map?

____

____

2. How many rivers are shown on the map? _______________

Tuesday

1. Which states does the Arkansas River run through?

____

____

2. Which river runs through Alaska?

____

Wednesday

1. Name the oceans that border the U.S.

____

2. Which two states share the Columbia River?

____

Waterways of the United States

Thursday

1. Name three of the Great Lakes.

   ____

   ____

2. The St. Lawrence River flows out of which lake?

   ____

Friday

1. Name three of the states that share the Colorado River.

   ____

2. Which three rivers on this map flow into the Mississippi River?

   ____

Challenge

- Trace all the rivers in dark blue.
- Color the Great Lakes light blue.
- Color the oceans and the Gulf of Mexico blue-green.

A Physical Map: Colorado

WEEK 14

Monday

1. Name the large mountain range in Colorado.

____

2. Which landform is in the eastern part of Colorado?

____

Tuesday

1. How many rivers are shown on the map?

____

2. Which river is found in southern Colorado?

____

Wednesday

1. How many tall mountain peaks are shown on the map?

____

2. Which mountain peak is the highest? How high is it?

____

A Physical Map: Colorado

Thursday

1. Are the Rocky Mountains east or west of the capital?

   ____

2. Which river runs through the northeast part of Colorado?

   ____

Friday

1. Which activity would people most likely do in the Rocky
   Mountains—snow ski or water ski?

   ____

2. Which is most likely found in the Great Plains—wheat fields or
   gold mines?

   ____

Challenge

Colorado has 11 national forests. They are mostly in the western
half of the state. On the map, draw several trees west of Denver.
Draw a picture of a tree and write the word **forest** in the map key.

    Daily Geography Practice • EMC 6853 • © Evan-Moor Corporation

A Physical Map: Arizona

Monday

1. Name three kinds of landforms in Arizona.

____

2. Which river runs by the capital city of Phoenix?

____

Tuesday

1. What is the name of the most famous canyon in Arizona?

____

2. In which part of Arizona is Canyon de Chelly?

____

Wednesday

1. Which desert is south of the Gila River?

____

2. Which desert is located south of the Little Colorado River?

____

A Physical Map: Arizona

Thursday

1. In which part of the state is the Grand Canyon located?

   ____

2. Which river lies at the base of the Grand Canyon?

   ____

Friday

1. What is Arizona's nickname?

   ____

2. Name a state or country that borders Arizona.

   ____

Challenge

The Grand Canyon and the Painted Desert are very colorful. Color
the Grand Canyon and the Painted Desert in shades of yellow,
brown, red, and pink.

A Physical Map: Minnesota

Monday

1. Name two of the lakes on the map.

____

2. Name two of the rivers on the map.

____

Tuesday

1. The Mississippi River begins at which lake?

____

2. Does the Mississippi River run north and south, or east and west?

____

Wednesday

1. Which waterfall is located near Two Harbors?

____

2. Lake of the Woods is between Minnesota and which country?

____

A Physical Map: Minnesota

Thursday

1. Which large lake borders northeast Minnesota?

____

2. Which lake is between the Mississippi and St. Croix Rivers?

____

Friday

1. Where is the Red River located?

____

____

2. What is Minnesota's nickname?

____

Challenge

Color all the lakes on the map light blue. Trace all the rivers in dark blue.

Daily Geography Practice • EMC 6853 • © Evan-Moor Corporation

A Physical Map: Massachusetts

WEEK 17

Monday

1. Which ocean borders Massachusetts?

2. Which three bays are shown on this map?

Tuesday

1. Which two islands are named on this map?

2. What is the capital of Massachusetts? Which bay is near the capital city?

Wednesday

1. Which two rivers flow into the Atlantic Ocean?

2. Which two rivers are separated by mountains?

A Physical Map: Massachusetts

Thursday

1. Name the peninsula on this map.

2. Name the city located at the tip of the peninsula.

Friday

1. What is the coastline of Massachusetts like?

2. Which waterway is between Cape Cod and Martha's Vineyard?

Challenge

On the map page, color the coastline of Massachusetts brown.
Trace the rivers in dark blue. Color the Atlantic Ocean with its
bays and sound light blue.

Daily Geography Practice • EMC 6853 • © Evan-Moor Corporation

A Physical Map: Hawaii

Monday

1. Hawaii is made up of how many islands? How many main islands are there?

   ____

2. In which ocean is Hawaii located? ___________________________

Tuesday

1. What is the capital of Hawaii? On which island is the capital found?

   ____

2. What is the name of the largest island in size?

   ____

Wednesday

1. Which three islands are closest to Maui?

   ____

   ____

2. Which main island is smallest in size?

   ____

A Physical Map: Hawaii

Thursday

1. In which direction is Hawaii from the mainland of the U.S.?

   ____

2. How far away is the state of Hawaii from the mainland of
   the U.S.?

   ____

Friday

1. How many main islands are northwest of Oahu? How many main
   islands are southeast of Oahu?

   ____

2. Name the two volcanoes on the map. Which one is the most
   active?

   ____

Challenge

On the map page, write the definition of a volcano. Draw a picture
of a volcano erupting. Use a picture dictionary to help you.

     Daily Geography Practice • EMC 6853 • © Evan-Moor Corporation

The Pacific Region of the United States

Monday

1. How many states are in the Pacific Region?

   ____

2. Which ocean do all the states border?

   ____

Tuesday

1. Which three states in the Pacific Region touch other U.S. states?

   ____

2. Which state is made up of all islands?

   ____

Wednesday

1. Which states share a border with Oregon?

   ____

2. Which states are north of California?

   ____

The Pacific Region
of the United States

Thursday

1. Which states border Canada?

____

2. Which state borders Mexico? _________________________

Friday

1. Which state is the largest in land area? Which two oceans border the state?

____

2. Which state is farthest north? Which state is farthest south?

____

Challenge

Part 1: Draw a line from the state to its capital. The first one has been completed for you. Use a United States map to help you.

State	Capital
Alaska	Salem
California	Olympia
Hawaii	Sacramento
Oregon	Juneau
Washington	Honolulu

Part 2: On the map, write the name of each capital next to the star on each state.

The Southwest Region of the United States

Monday

1. How many states are in the Southwest region?

____

2. Which states are in the Southwest region?

____

____

Tuesday

1. Which state is the largest in size?

____

2. Are the southwest states closer to Canada or Mexico?

____

Wednesday

1. Which southwest states border Oklahoma?

____

2. Which southwest state does <u>not</u> share a border with Mexico?

____

The Southwest Region of the United States

Thursday

1. Which state has the longest border with Mexico? _______________

2. Which state borders California, New Mexico, Nevada, and Utah?

____

Friday

1. Name all the borders of Texas that are labeled on the map.

____

____

2. Why are Arizona, New Mexico, Oklahoma, and Texas called a region?

____

Challenge

Part 1: Draw a line from the state to its capital. The first one has been completed for you. Use a United States map to help you.

State	Capital
Arizona	Oklahoma City
New Mexico	Phoenix
Oklahoma	Austin
Texas	Santa Fe

Part 2: On the map, write the name of each capital next to the star on each state.

The Northeast Region of the United States

Monday

1. How many states are in the Northeast region?

____

2. Name the three largest states in size.

____

Tuesday

1. Which ocean borders seven of the states in the Northeast region?

____

2. Which country is north of the Northeast region of the U.S.?

____

Wednesday

1. Pennsylvania borders which states in the Northeast?

____

2. Which state borders both Lake Erie and Lake Ontario?

____

The Northeast Region of the United States

Thursday

1. Which state is the smallest in size? ______________________

2. Which state borders Canada and only one U.S. state?

   ____

Friday

1. Name three of the five states that border Massachusetts.

   ____

2. Name three states that border the Atlantic Ocean.

   ____

Challenge

Part 1: Match each capital with each state. The first three have been completed for you. Use a United States map to help you name the others.

State		Capital	
1. Connecticut	d	a.	Albany
2. Maine	c	b.	Harrisburg
3. Massachusetts	h	c.	Augusta
4. New Hampshire	____	d.	Hartford
5. New Jersey	____	e.	Montpelier
6. New York	____	f.	Concord
7. Pennsylvania	____	g.	Providence
8. Rhode Island	____	h.	Boston
9. Vermont	____	i.	Trenton

Part 2: On the map, write the name of each capital next to the star on each state.

     Daily Geography Practice • EMC 6853 • © Evan-Moor Corporation

The Southeast Region of the United States

Monday

1. How many states are in the Southeast region? _______________

2. Name three states that border the Atlantic Ocean.

____

Tuesday

1. Name the four states that border the Gulf of Mexico.

____

____

2. Name the two states that are farthest west.

____

Wednesday

1. What is the name of the capital of the United States?

____

2. Where is the capital of the United States located?

____

The Southeast Region of the United States

Thursday

1. Which four states do <u>not</u> border any labeled waterway?

   ____

2. How many states share a border with Alabama? ___________

Friday

1. Which state is a large peninsula with small islands off its coast?

   ____

2. Which two states are located in the northeast tip of the Southeast region?

   ____

Challenge

Five state capitals are labeled on the map of the Southeast region. Nine are not labeled. Write the names of the nine capitals on the correct states. Use a United States map to help you with the names.

Capitals

Baton Rouge	Little Rock	Raleigh
Columbia	Montgomery	Atlanta
Jackson	Nashville	Tallahassee

The Statue of Liberty

Monday

1. Describe what the Statue of Liberty is wearing.

____

____

2. Which two items is Lady Liberty holding?

____

Tuesday

1. The Statue of Liberty stands on which island?

____

2. The Statue of Liberty is located in which harbor?

____

Wednesday

1. How tall is the Statue of Liberty?

____

2. How tall is the base that the statue stands on?

____

The Statue of Liberty

Thursday

1. In which city and state is the Statue of Liberty located?

____

2. What is another name for the Statue of Liberty?

____

Friday

1. Which word means the same as "liberty"—**freedom**, **joy**, or **friendship**?

____

2. Why is the Statue of Liberty important to the United States?

____

____

Challenge

To visit the Statue of Liberty, people take a ferry. On the map, draw a ferry going to the Statue of Liberty.

The White House

WEEK 24

Monday

1. Who lives and works in the White House?

____

2. What is the address of the White House?

____

Tuesday

1. Is there an office building or a park south of the White House?

____

2. Which building is next to the White House in square A3?

____

Wednesday

1. What is the Ellipse? In which square is the Ellipse?

____

2. Which building is to the east of the Ellipse?

____

The White House

Thursday

1. Where would a tourist see different kinds of fish? In which square is that building?

   ____

2. Where would a tourist see displays of America's past? In which square is that building?

   ____

Friday

1. How is George Washington, the first president, honored in the nation's capital?

   ____

   ____

2. Which cultural landmark is located in square C1?

   ____

Challenge

In square B1 on the map, draw your favorite symbol of America. Remember, it should be found in Washington, D.C.

A Weather Map

Monday

1. How many states are shown on the map?

____

2. In which region of the United States are the states located?

____

Tuesday

1. What is the weather like in Kansas?

____

2. What is the weather like in Nebraska?

____

Wednesday

1. What is the weather like in Wisconsin and Michigan?

____

2. In which state is it snowing?

____

A Weather Map

Thursday

1. Which state is 40° and partly cloudy? Which state is south of this
   state?

   ____

2. Which two states have temperatures of 60° and rain?

   ____

Friday

1. How many states border the Great Lakes?

   ____

2. Which state has the lowest temperature? Which state has the
   highest temperature?

   ____

Challenge

Choose which state in the North-Central region you would like
to visit. On the map page, write about the weather in that state.
Then write about the kinds of activities you could do in that kind of
weather.

Oregon's Forests

Monday

1. Oregon has many mountains and _______________________.

2. Do forests cover one-half or all of Oregon?

____

Tuesday

1. Name three kinds of trees that grow in Oregon.

____

2. Name three kinds of animals that live in the forest.

____

Wednesday

1. Are most of the forests near mountains in Oregon?

____

2. Which mountains are in northeast Oregon? Are there forests in this area, too?

____

____

Oregon's Forests

Thursday

1. What is the state tree of Oregon?

   ____

2. How many national forests are in Oregon?

   ____

Friday

1. Eugene, Portland, and Salem are all on which river? What landforms are near the three cities?

   ____

   ____

2. Which states border Oregon? Do you think those states have forests?

   ____

Challenge

On the map, color the forests green. Choose an animal from the list and draw it on the map.

Ten Largest Cities in Wyoming

Monday

1. What does the map show?

2. What does the chart show?

Tuesday

1. What is the capital of Wyoming?

2. Is the capital the largest or smallest city?

Wednesday

1. Which city has a population of 17,444? Is it north or south of the capital?

2. Which city and river have the same name? What is the city's population?

Ten Largest Cities in Wyoming

Thursday

1. Is Evanston's population more or less than 12,000?

2. Which city has a population of 10,615? Which river is it on?

Friday

1. Which city is the second largest in population? Which river is it on?

2. Which two cities have the smallest populations?

Challenge

On the map, number the three largest cities from largest to smallest in population. For example, Cheyenne is #1.

A County Fair

Monday

1. What is the title of the map?

____

2. Name three areas at the county fair.

____

Tuesday

1. Name the area that has fun rides.

____

2. Which games are in the game area?

____

Wednesday

1. Name three kinds of animals that are at the county fair.

____

2. What things have people made to show at the fair?

____

A County Fair

Thursday

1. Who is performing next at the Grandstand?

   ____

2. Where can you eat at the fair?

   ____

Friday

1. Which rides cost 3 tickets?

   ____

2. Which ride costs the most tickets?

   ____

Challenge

Which part at the county fair is your favorite? On the back of the map, write about your favorite part of the county fair and tell why you like it.

A Product Map: Wisconsin

Monday

1. How many areas of Wisconsin have dairy farms?

   ____

2. Name two dairy products made from milk.

   ____

Tuesday

1. Are most of the dairy farm areas east or west of the Wisconsin River?

   ____

2. How many dairy farms are in Wisconsin?

   ____

Wednesday

1. Each dairy farm has about how many dairy cows?

   ____

2. How much milk does a dairy cow produce in one year?

   ____

A Product Map: Wisconsin

Thursday

1. What is Wisconsin's nickname?

   ____

2. Which three cities are east of the Wisconsin River? Which city
   has more dairy farms near it?

   ____

   ____

Friday

1. _______________ pounds of milk make 2 pounds of cheese.

2. _______________ pounds of milk make 2 pounds of butter.

Challenge

The three main dairy products are milk, cheese, and butter. Draw
a milk carton, a block of cheese, and a stick of butter near the
facts on the map.

Living in a Community

Monday

1. How many different types of homes are shown on this map?

____

2. On which street are the Pearl Homes located?

____

Tuesday

1. What is the name of the apartment building on Green Avenue?

____

2. What is the address of the apartment building?

____

Wednesday

1. On which street are the Tree Top Homes?

____

2. What are the addresses for the Tree Top Homes?

____

Living in a Community

Thursday

1. Which type of homes are located at 12 H–15 H First Street?

2. Which type of homes are located at 10–12 Brown Avenue?

Friday

1. On which street are the Corner Homes located?

2. What are the addresses of the Pearl Homes?

Challenge

Which kind of house would you like to live in? On the map, write about your favorite kind of house and tell why you like it.

Community Services

Monday

1. A community provides ________________________________ for its people.

2. Which community services have entrances on Safety Street?

   ____

   ____

Tuesday

1. Which community services are located on Express Street?

   ____

   ____

2. What is the address of the police station?

   ____

Wednesday

1. What is the address of the hospital?

   ____

2. On which street can you mail a letter?

   ____

Community Services

Thursday

1. The park is a community service also. On which street is the park located?

   ____

2. The courthouse is located on the corner of Second Avenue and

   ____ .

Friday

1. Which community service helps you get around town?

   ____

2. How many community services are shown on this map?

   ____

Challenge

Color the community services on the map that handle emergencies.

     Daily Geography Practice • EMC 6853 • © Evan-Moor Corporation

The Bluegrass Region of Kentucky

Monday

1. Which region in Kentucky has many horse farms?

   ____

2. In which part of the state is this region?

   ____

Tuesday

1. Which two rivers border the Bluegrass Region?

   ____

2. Which mountains are southeast of the Bluegrass Region?

   ____

Wednesday

1. What is the capital of Kentucky? On which river is it located?

   ____

2. Which cities on the map are located in the Bluegrass Region?

   ____

The Bluegrass Region of Kentucky

Thursday

1. What is special about the horses in the Bluegrass Region?

2. What special event happens in Louisville every year?

Friday

1. Which season of the year does the grass look more blue-green?

2. Which rivers in Kentucky are <u>not</u> located in the Bluegrass Region?

Challenge

Lexington is called the "horse capital of the world." On the map, color the Bluegrass Region blue-green.

A Tourist Map: California

WEEK 33

Monday

1. Which state is shown on the map?

____

2. Which ocean is shown on the map?

____

Tuesday

1. Name two tourist attractions south of San Francisco.

____

2. Name two tourist attractions north of San Francisco.

____

Wednesday

1. Which tourist attraction is in Monterey?

____

2. Name two things tourists could do in the Pacific Ocean.

____

A Tourist Map: California

Thursday

1. In which city is the Golden Gate Bridge located? Is the city on the coast or inland?

2. Which islands are located off the coast of California?

Friday

1. There is a famous zoo in which city? Is the city in the southern, central, or northern part of the state?

2. Which famous tourist attraction is located in Anaheim? Which cities are near Anaheim?

Challenge

California has beautiful mountains. The Coast Ranges are up and down the west coast of California. The Sierra Nevada Range is between Lake Tahoe and the Mojave Desert. Draw mountains in those two areas. Add the names of the mountains to the map.

Daily Geography Practice • EMC 6853 • © Evan-Moor Corporation

Minerals of Alaska

Monday

1. Name three minerals produced in Alaska.

2. How many gold mines are shown on the map?

Tuesday

1. Oil wells are near which two cities?

2. How much oil is produced in Alaska every day?

Wednesday

1. Which kind of gas does Alaska produce? In which part of Alaska is this gas found?

2. What is the capital of Alaska? Are there any mineral mines near there?

Minerals of Alaska

Thursday

1. In which area of Alaska are all three minerals found?

   ____

2. Which country borders Alaska? Which mineral is located along this border?

   ____

Friday

1. Name two minerals besides gold that are mined in Alaska.

   ____

2. Most of the gold deposits in Alaska are near which two cities?

   ____

Challenge

Color all the minerals on the map.

The Lewis and Clark Trail

Monday

1. A person who travels to discover new things is called

   ____ .

2. Which two men explored the western wilderness?

   ____

Tuesday

1. The explorers started their journey in which city?

   ____

2. Lewis and Clark traveled to which ocean?

   ____

Wednesday

1. In 1804, was most of the United States settled or still wilderness?

   ____

2. Which river did Lewis and Clark follow most of the way?

   ____

The Lewis and Clark Trail

Thursday

1. How many miles did Lewis and Clark travel?

   ____

2. In what year did they start their journey? In what year did
   it end?

   ____

Friday

1. What did Lewis and Clark discover?

   ____

2. What happened to the western wilderness after 1806?

   ____

   ____

Challenge

Meriwether Lewis kept journals. He wrote about animals, plants,
and people they saw along the trail. Pretend you were on the trail.
On the map page, write a journal entry about what you saw.

   Daily Geography Practice • EMC 6853 • © Evan-Moor Corporation

A Neighborhood Plan

Monday

1. What does the map show?

2. Name a place where children can play.

Tuesday

1. Is City Hall east or west of the car wash?

2. Are the A-Z Stores east or west of the fire station?

Wednesday

1. What is north of the park?

2. What is east of the park?

A Neighborhood Plan

Thursday

1. Which business is northeast of the vacant lot?

   ____

2. The city park is located on which three streets?

   ____

   ____

Friday

1. Which community services are shown on this map?

   ____

   ____

2. Name the businesses on the map.

   ____

Challenge

Think about places that you would find in a neighborhood. Decide what you would put in the vacant lot. Draw a picture in the vacant lot and label it.

 Daily Geography Practice • EMC 6853 • © Evan-Moor Corporation

What Is a Globe?

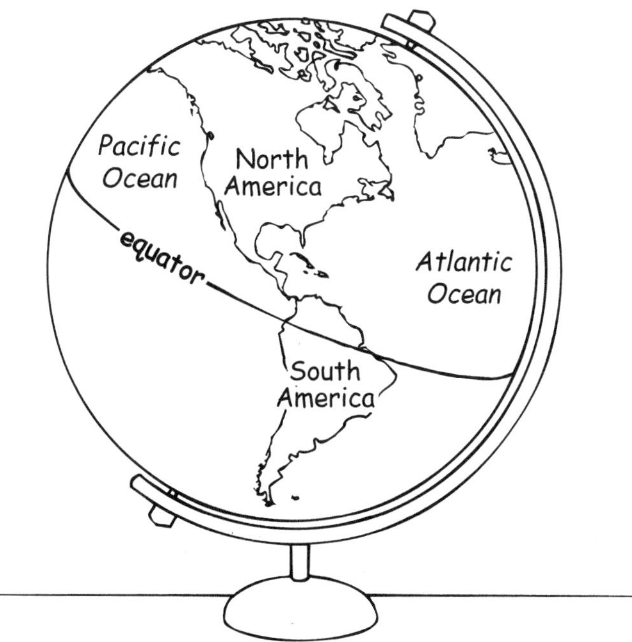

A globe is a model of Earth. It is shaped like a ball.

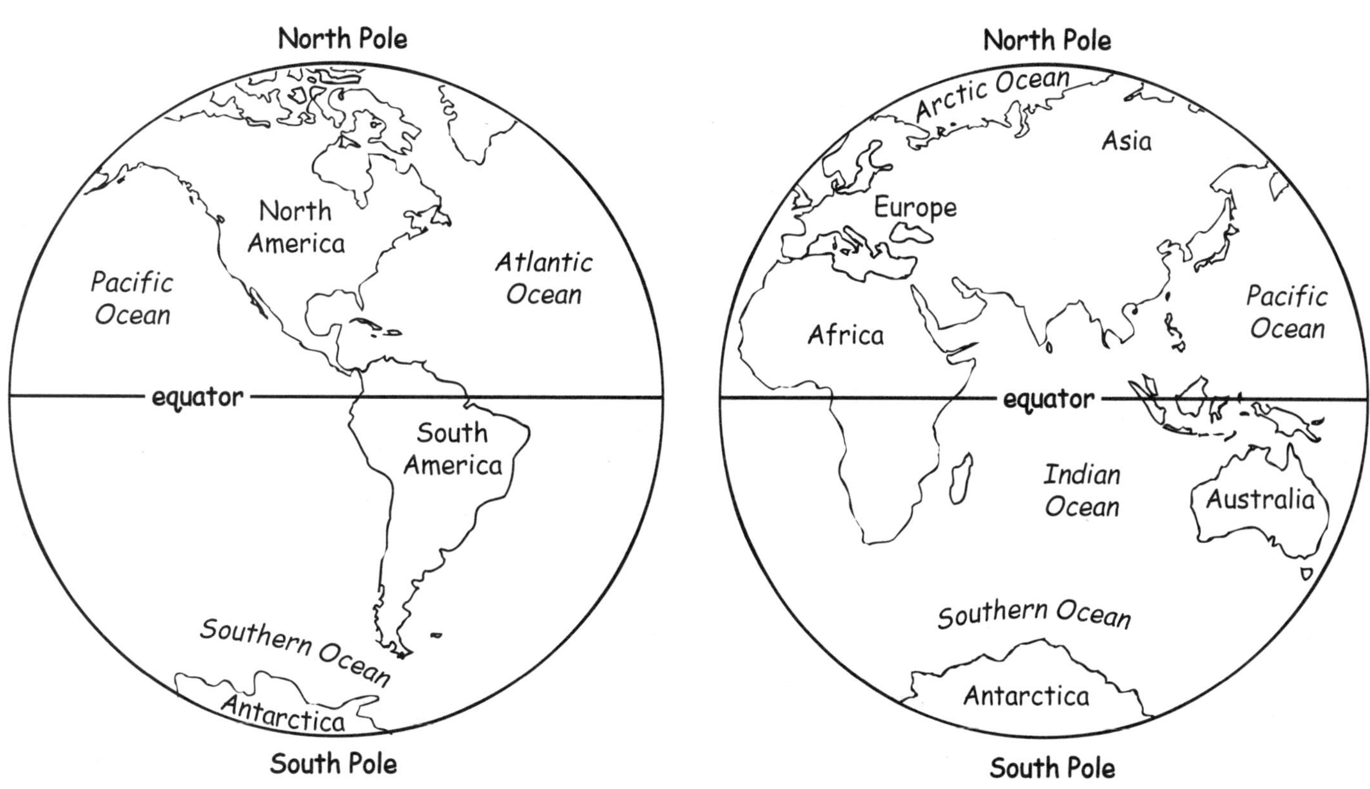

A globe shows an imaginary line called the equator.
The equator runs around the center of the Earth.

What Is a Map?

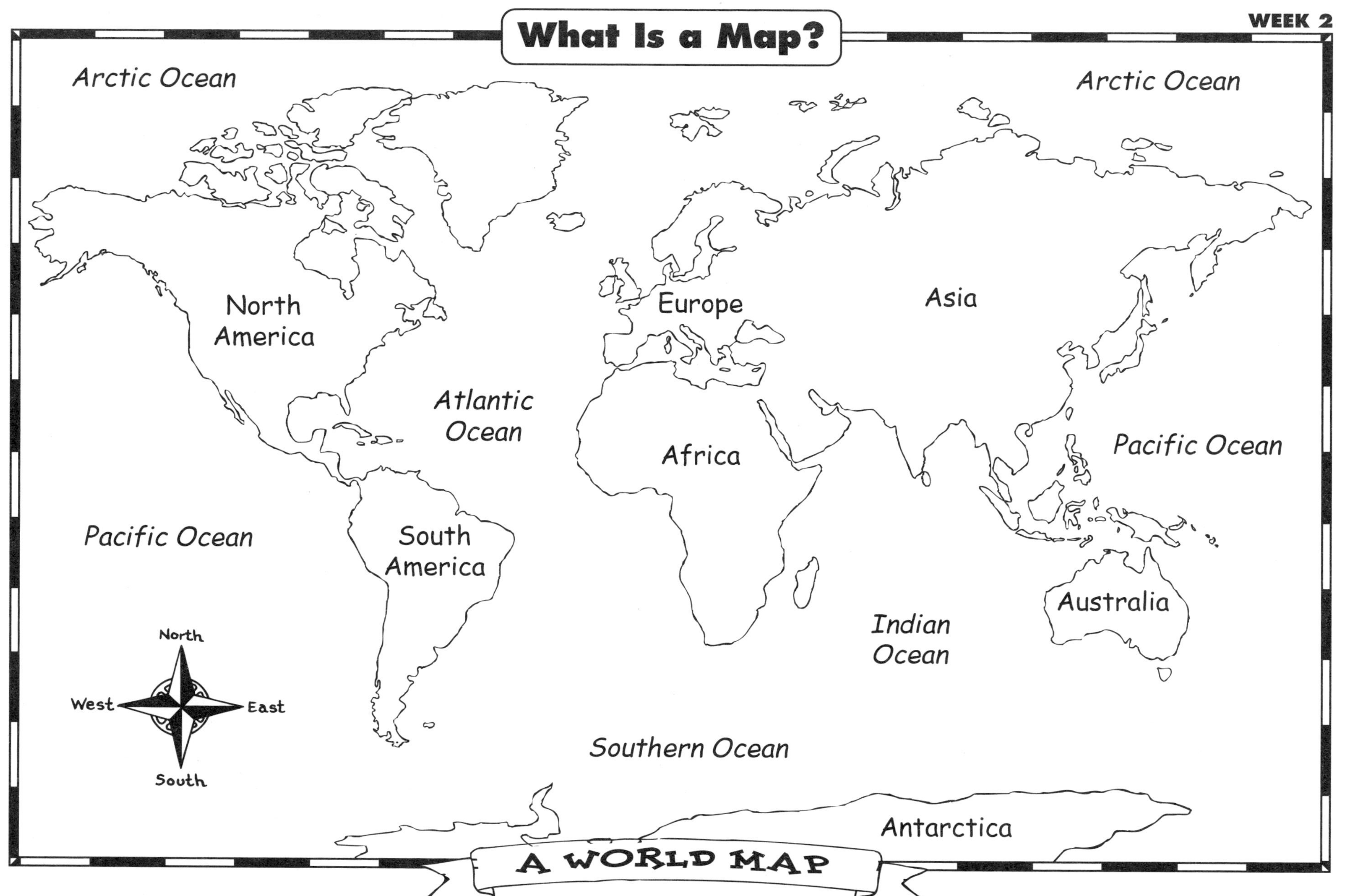

This map is a drawing of the world. It shows the seven continents. It also shows the five oceans.

Parts of a Map

The parts of the map include a title, a map key, and a compass rose.

This is the title. The title tells the name of the map.

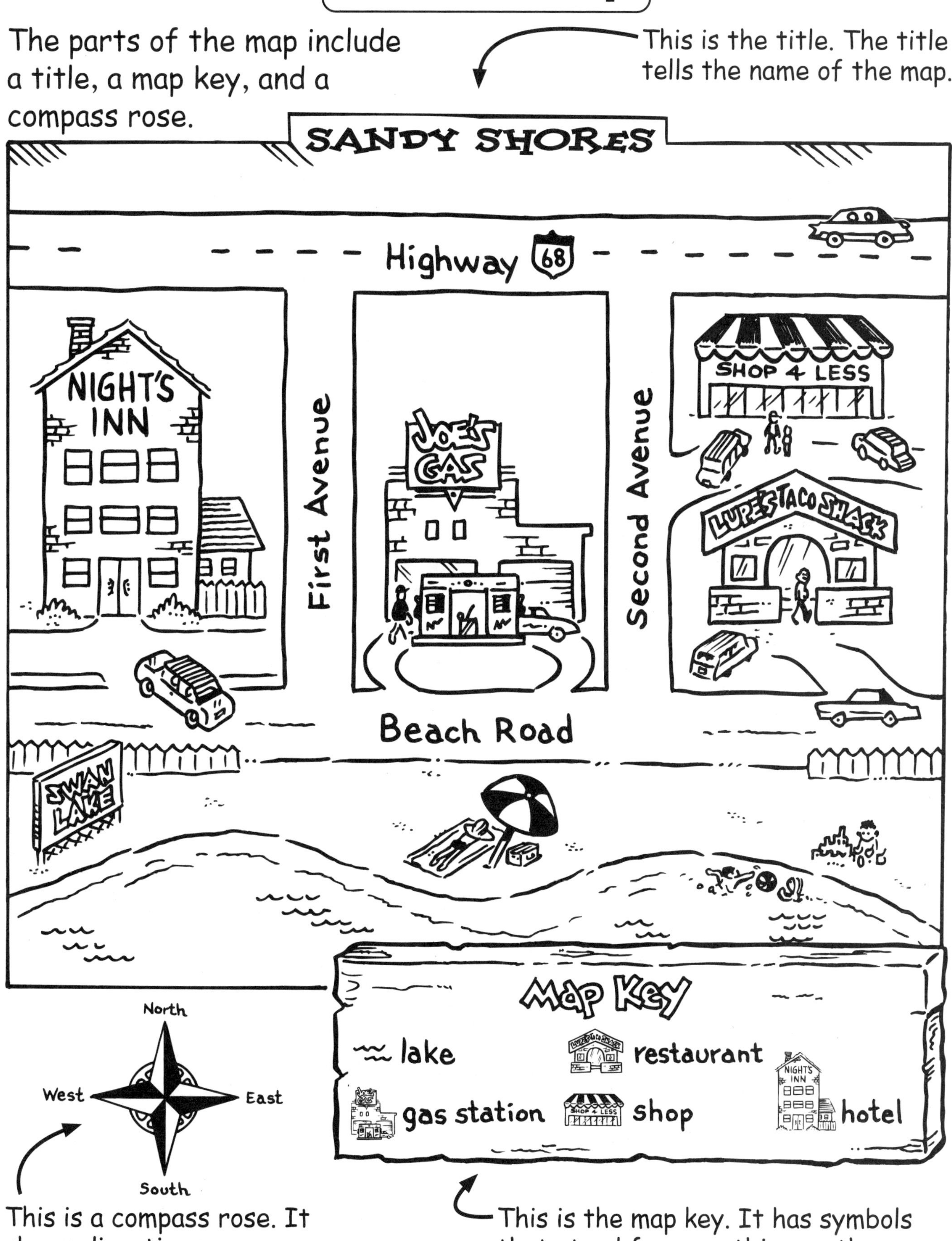

This is a compass rose. It shows directions on a map.

This is the map key. It has symbols that stand for something on the map.

Intermediate Directions

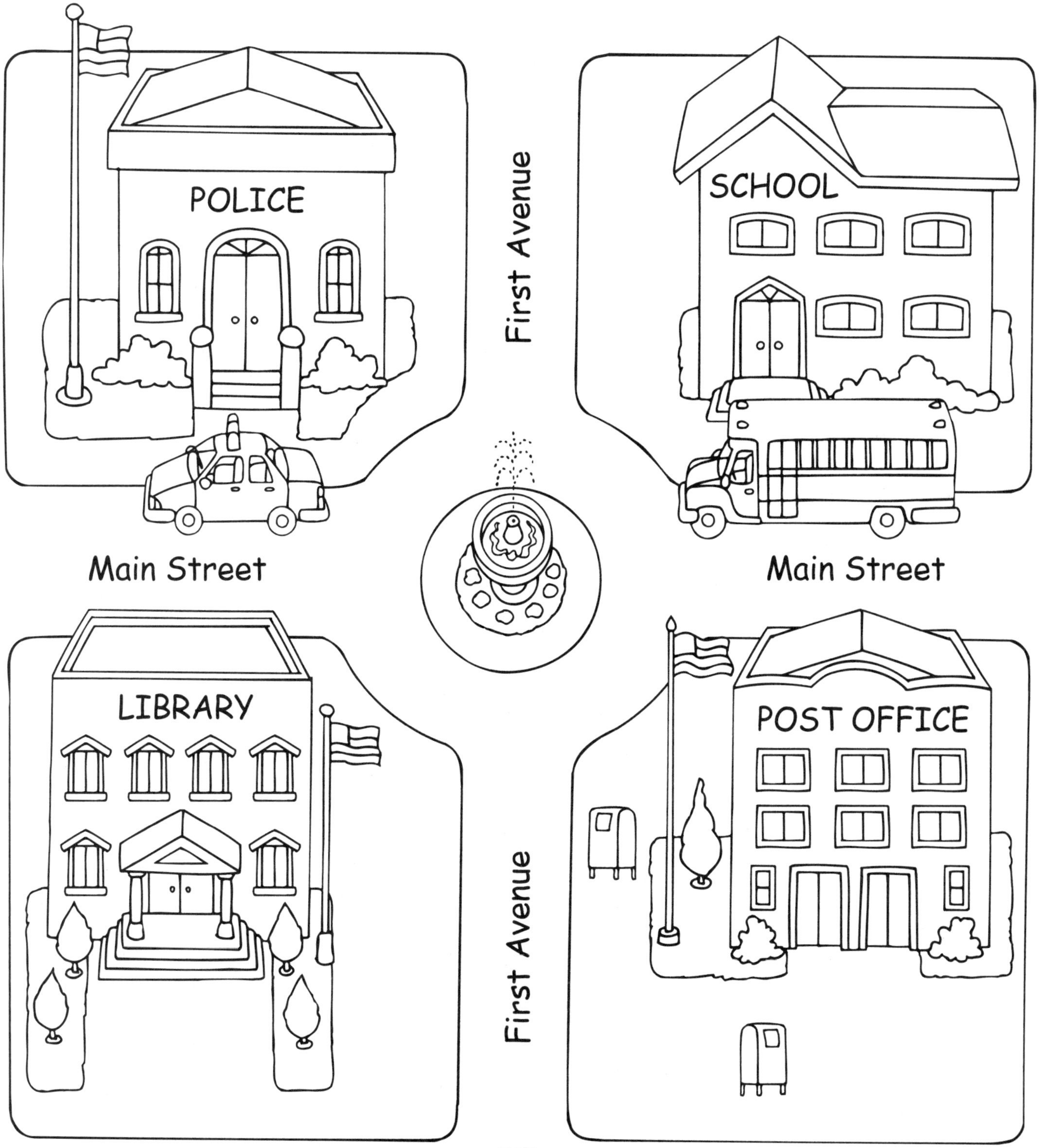
POLICE
SCHOOL
First Avenue
Main Street
Main Street
LIBRARY
POST OFFICE
First Avenue

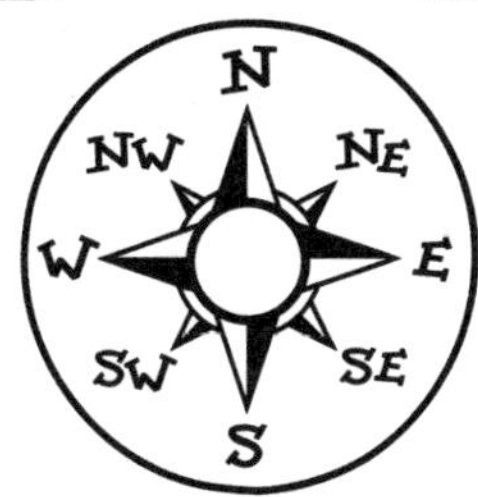

N, S, E, and W are cardinal directions.

N
NW
NE
W
E
SW
SE
S

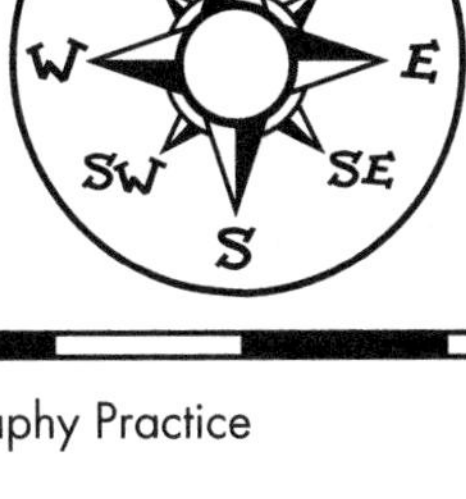

NE, NW, SE, and SW are the intermediate directions.

A Map Grid

1 2 3 4 5
A
B
C
D
E
ENTRANCE
KEY
Playground
Basketball
Picnic area
Water fountain
Baseball
Path
Park bench
Woods

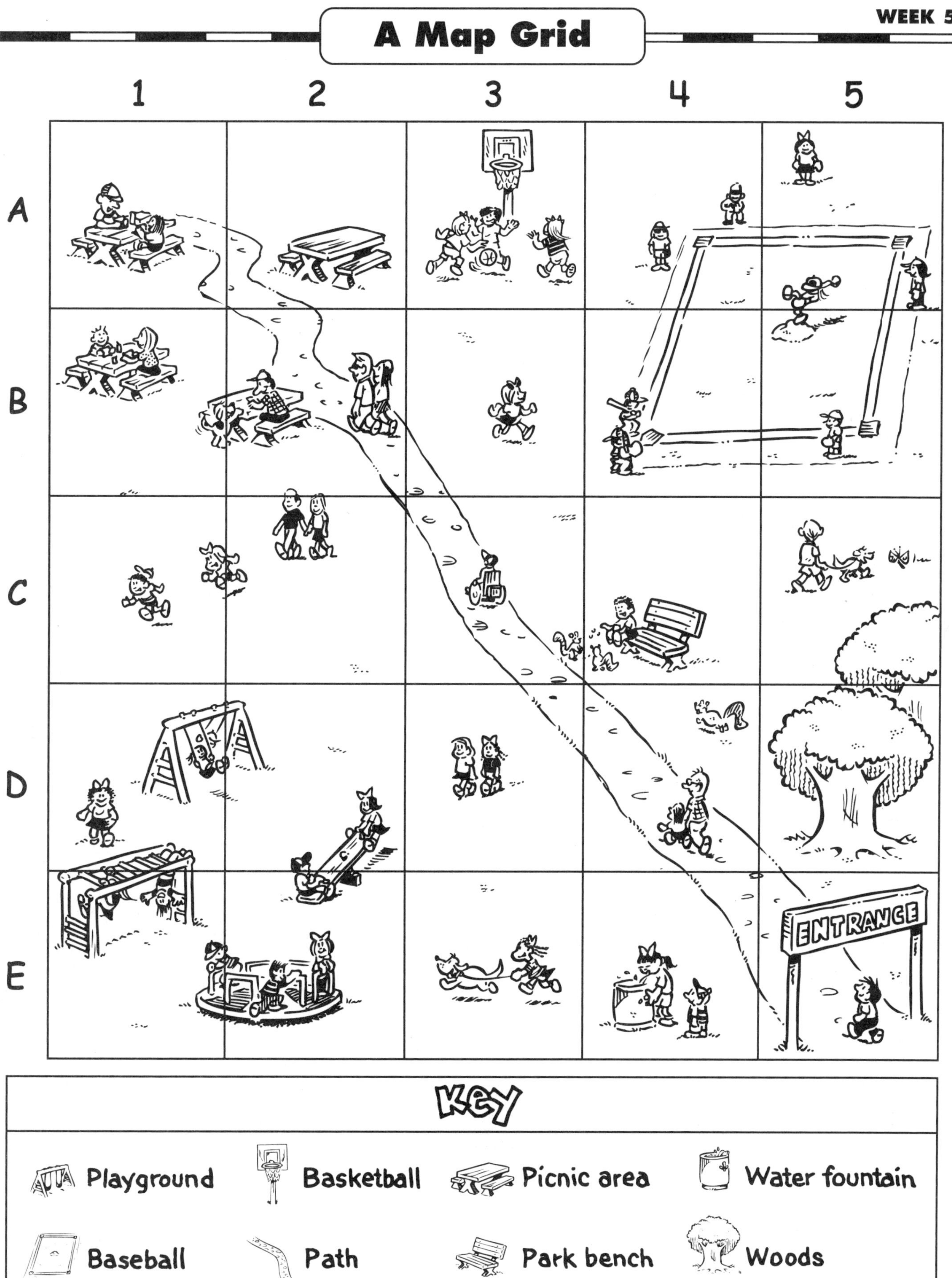

Alabama

1 2 3 4 5
A
B
C
D
E
F
G
Huntsville
Decatur
Gadsden
Birmingham
Tuscaloosa
Hoover
Auburn
Montgomery
Dothan
Mobile
Map Key
★ state capital
● city
-·-·- state border
N
W E
S
Index
Auburn D4
Birmingham C3
Decatur A3
Dothan F5
Gadsden........... B4
Hoover C3
Huntsville.......... A3
Mobile............. G1
Montgomery .. D3, D4
Tuscaloosa......... C2

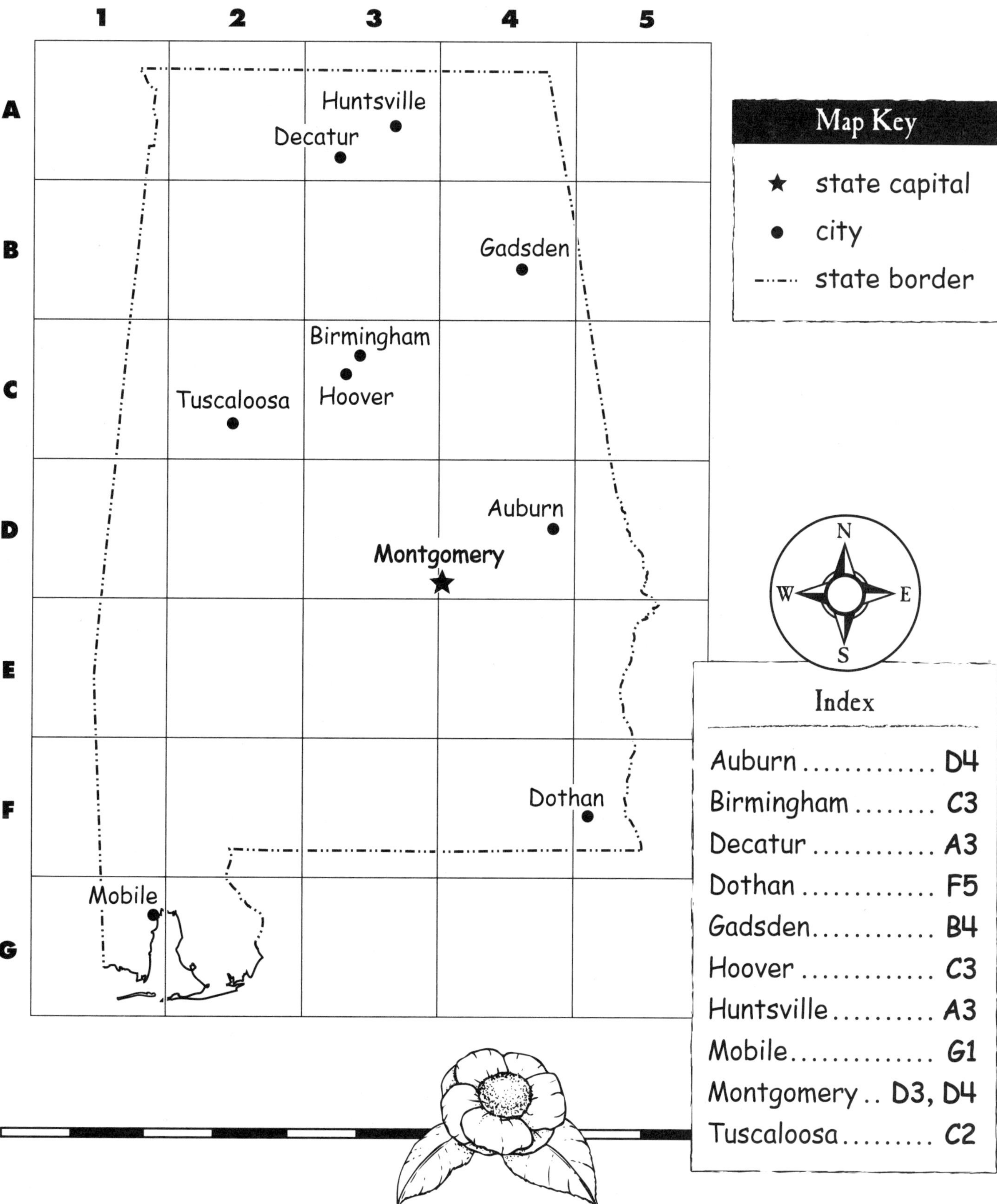

A Map Key

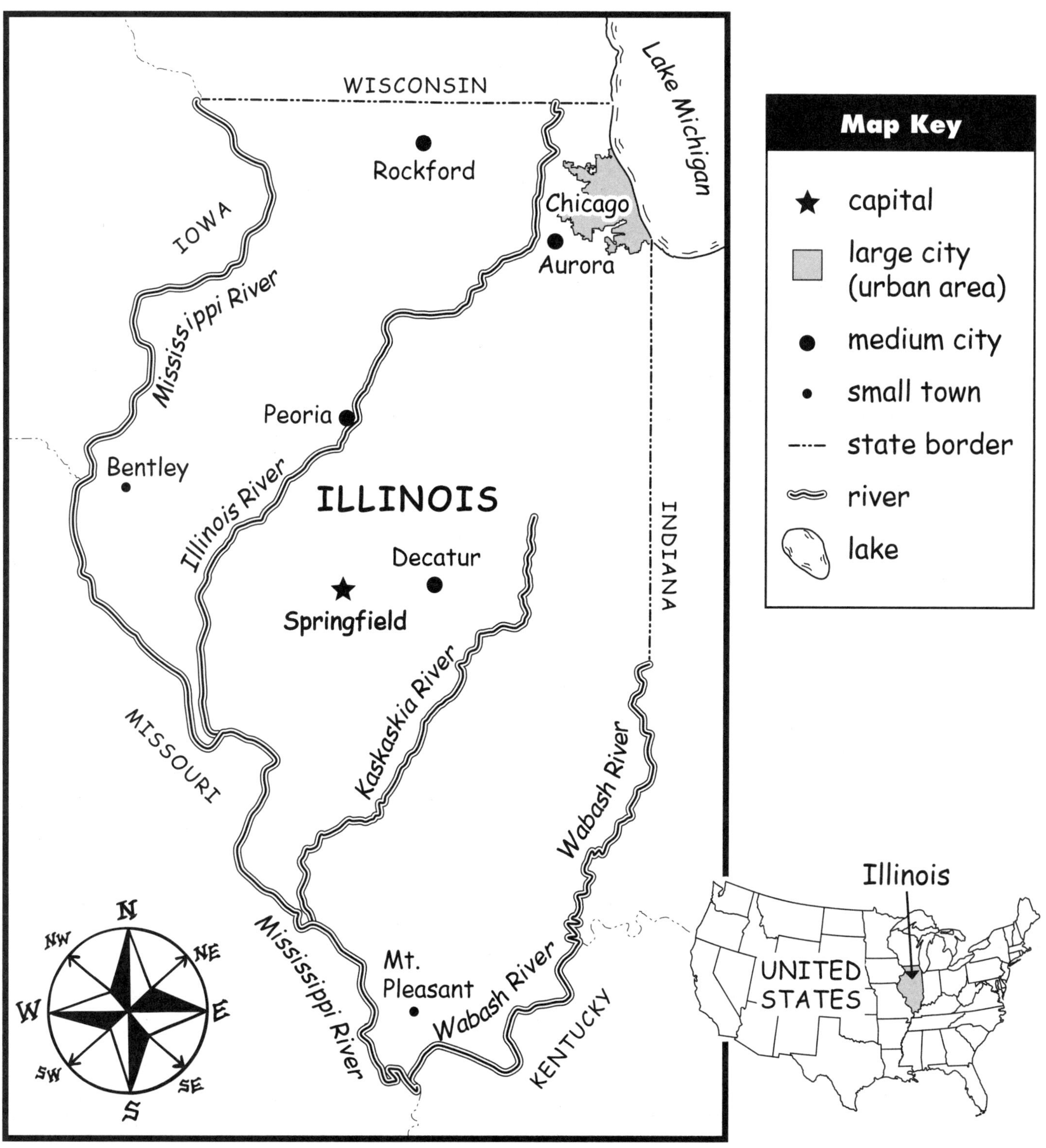

Can you name the states that border Illinois?

1. _________________________

2. _________________________

3. _________________________

4. _________________________

5. _________________________

A Map Scale

Map Key
★ capital
• city

TEXAS

Amarillo
El Paso
Midland
Abilene
Dallas
Austin
San Antonio
Houston
Corpus Christi
Brownsville

N
W E
S

Scale
0   100 miles
0   100 km
½ inch = 50 miles
1 inch = 100 miles
1½ inches = 150 miles
2 inches = 200 miles

Houston is about ______ miles from Brownsville.

Texas is the 2nd largest state in the United States.

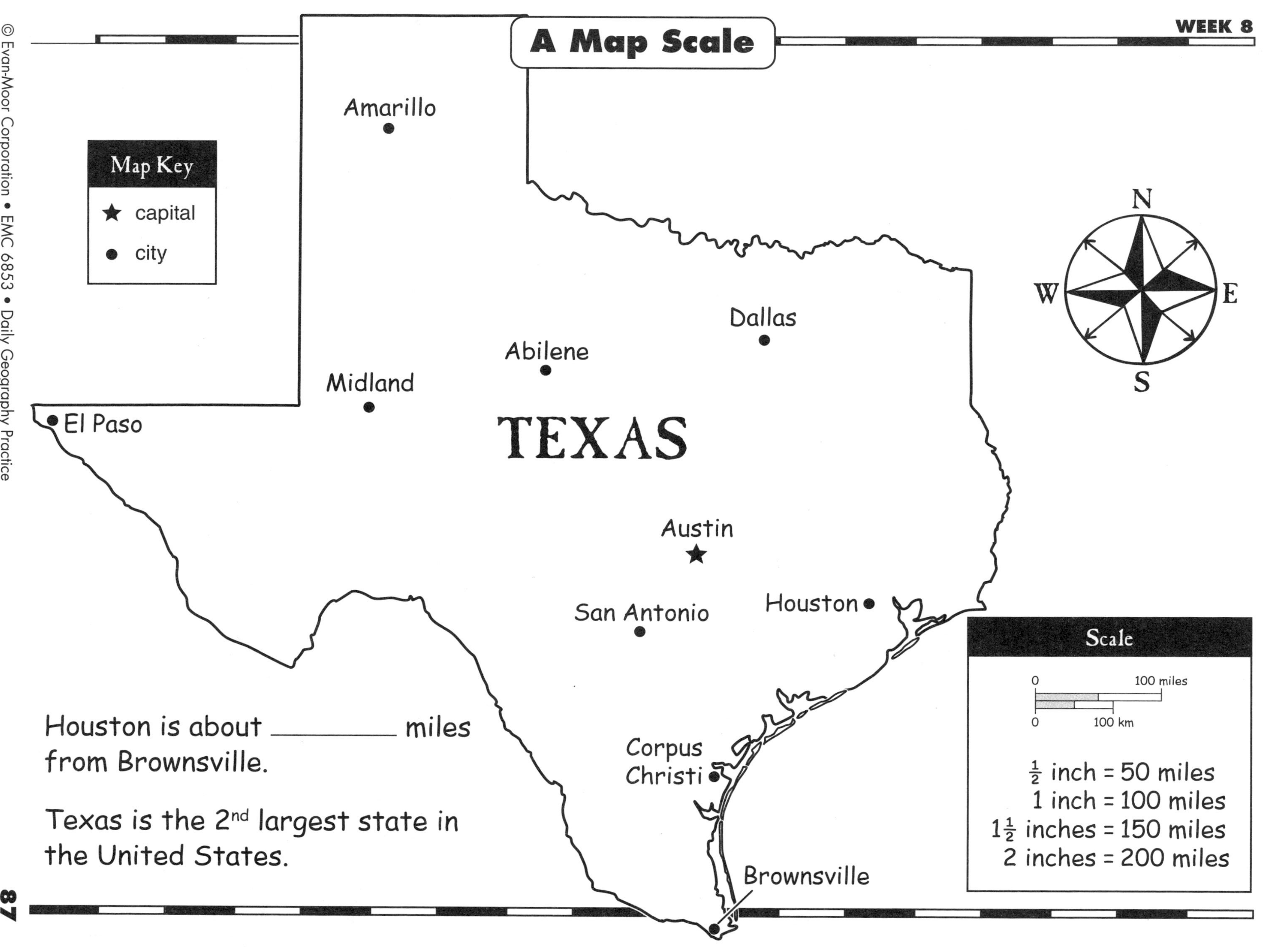

Picturing the United States

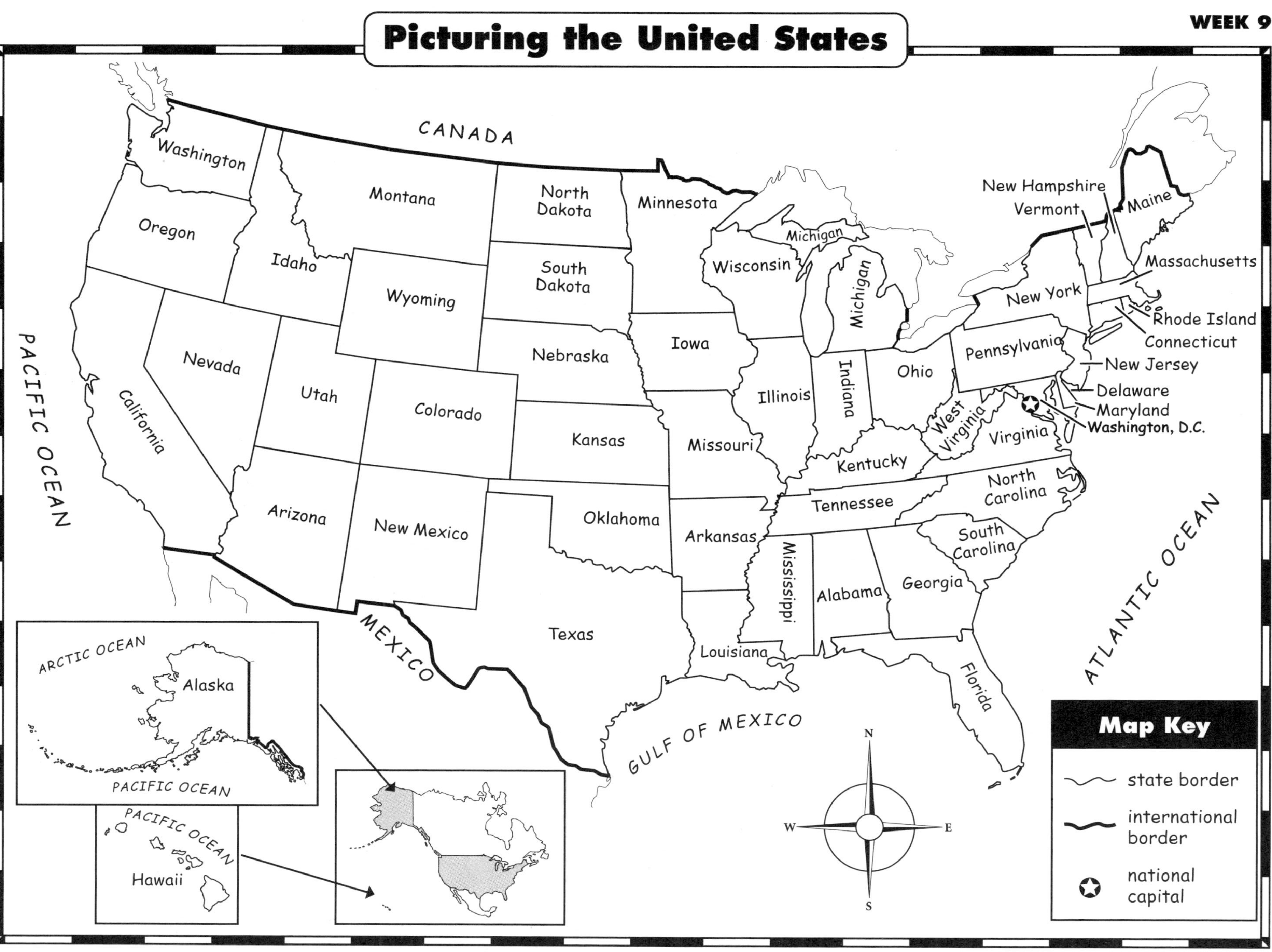

Picturing North America

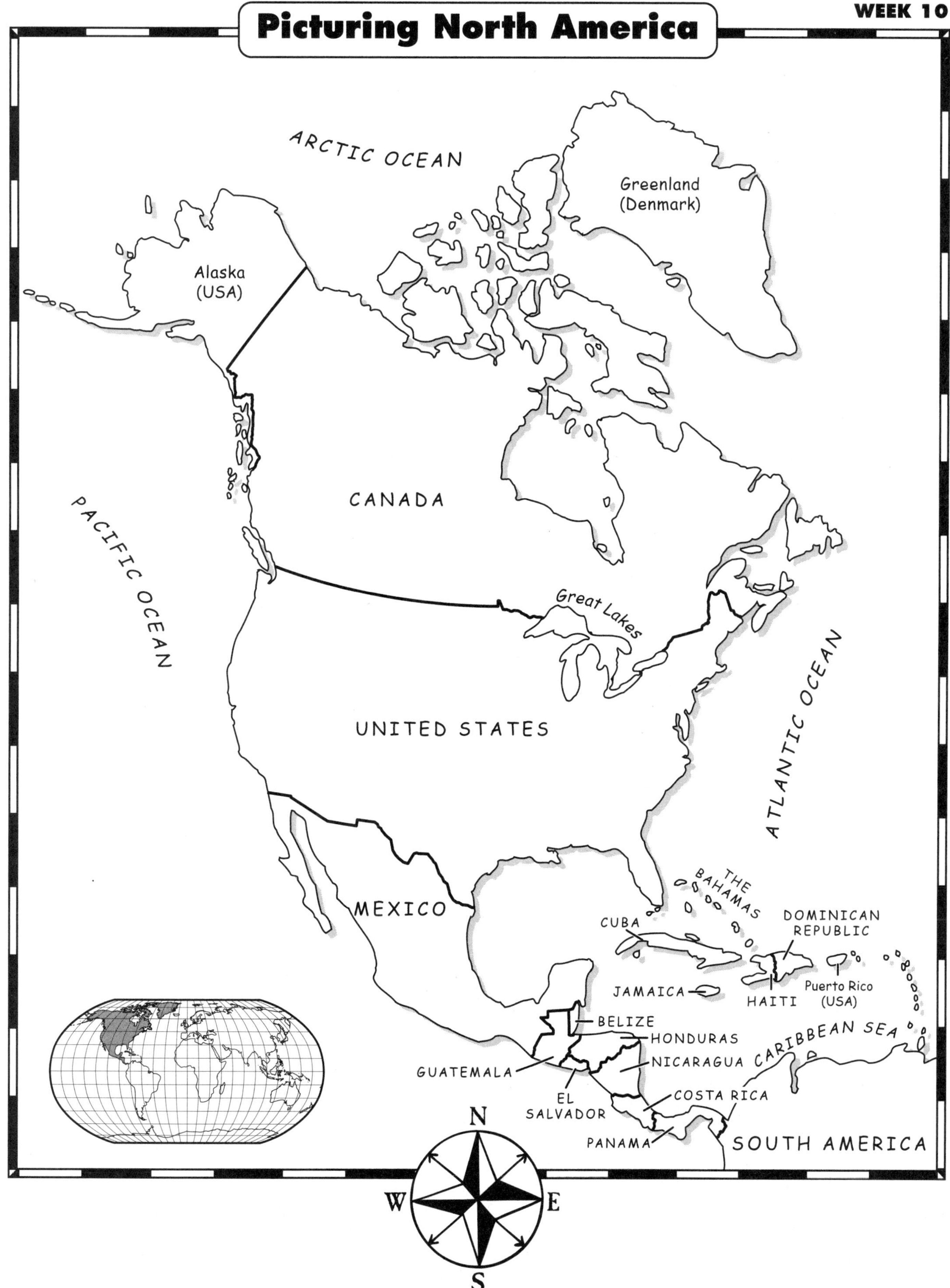

Transportation Routes in a Town

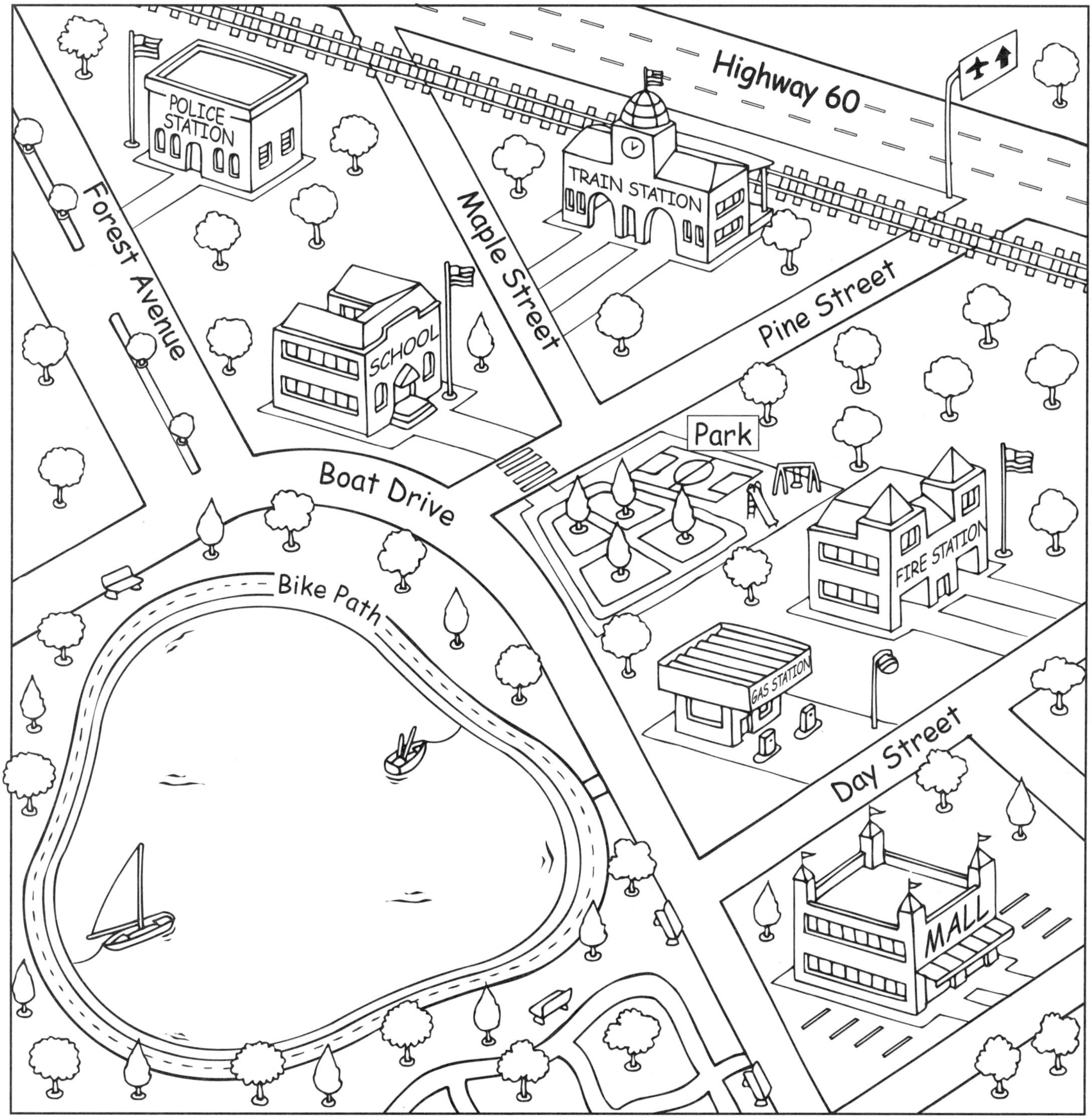

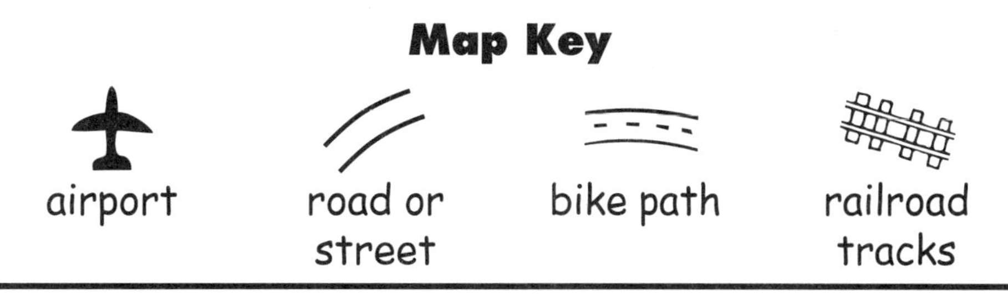

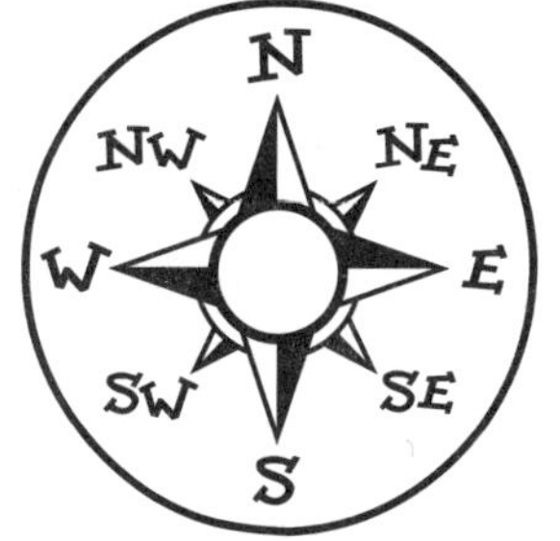

Map Key

| airport | road or street | bike path | railroad tracks |

A Road Map

ROAD MAP
South Dakota
South Dakota
Mobridge
Aberdeen
Spearfish
Pierre
Brookings
Rapid City
Mitchell
Sioux Falls
12
85
281
29
12
85
281
14
29
14
90
14
90
85
281
29
N
E
S
W
Map Key
90 interstate highway
12 U.S. highway
capital
city
state border

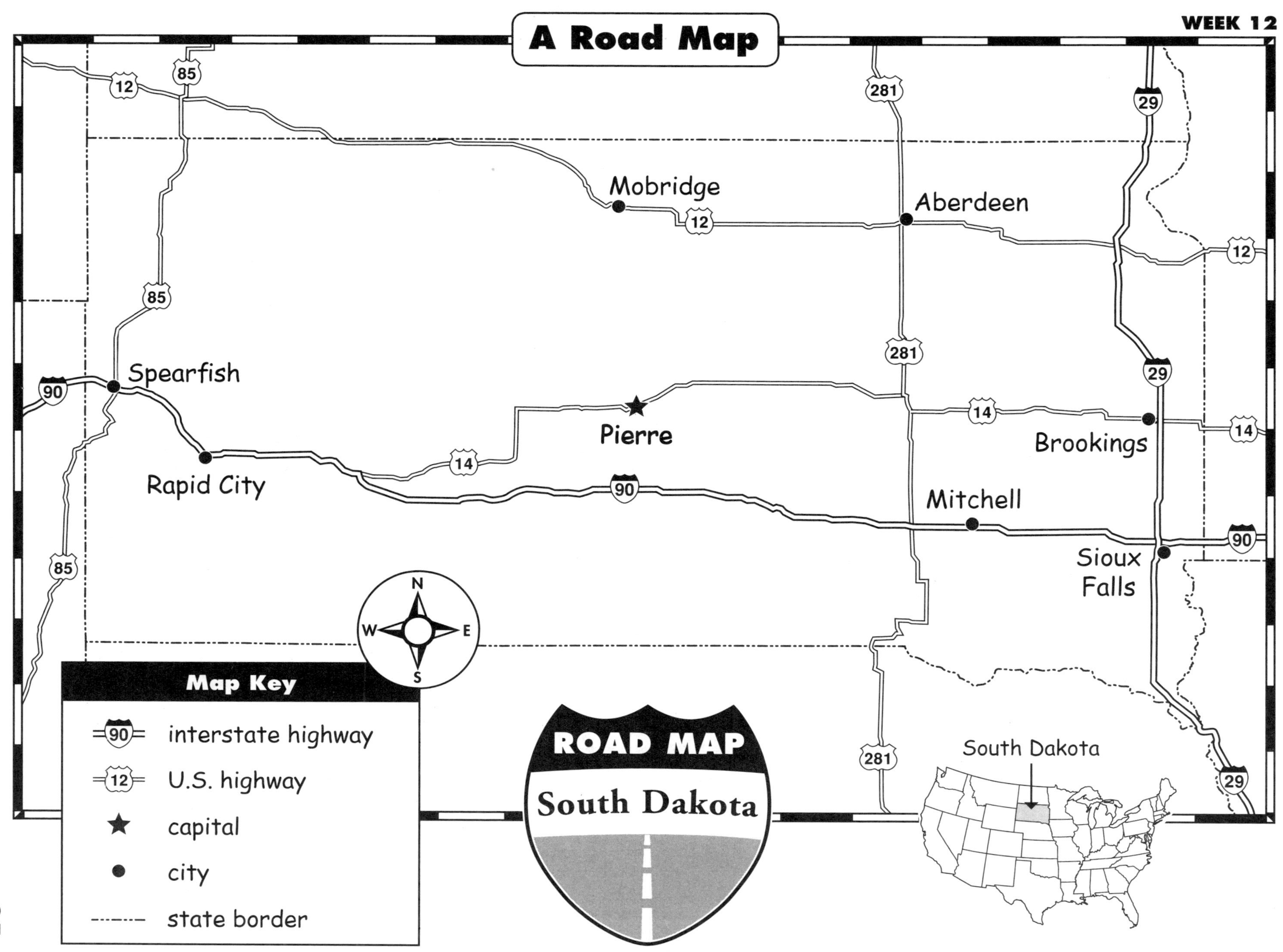

Waterways of the United States

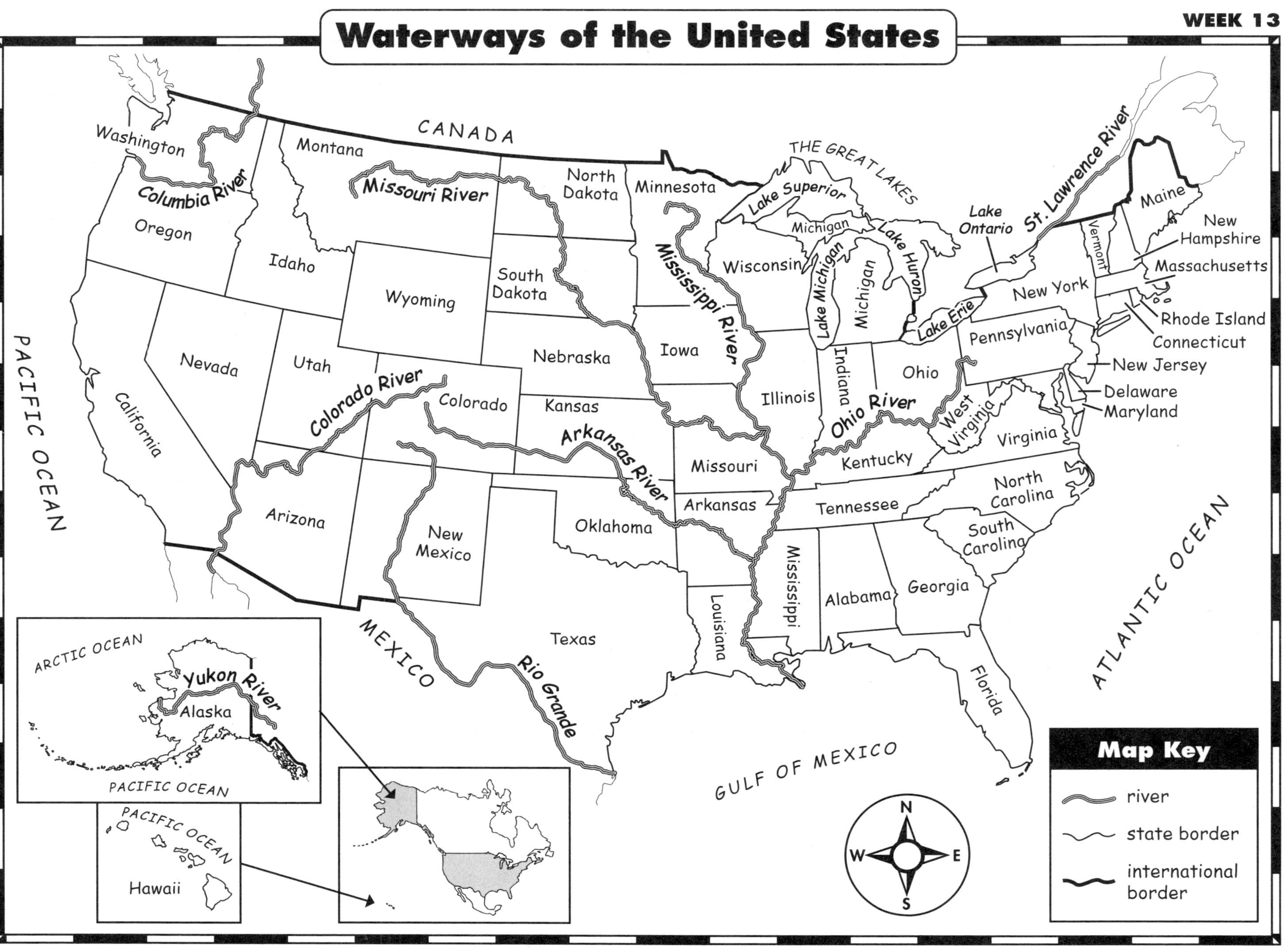

A Physical Map: Colorado

Colorado has more than 50 tall mountain peaks. Mount Elbert is the highest. It is 14,433 feet (4,399 m) high.

Colorado

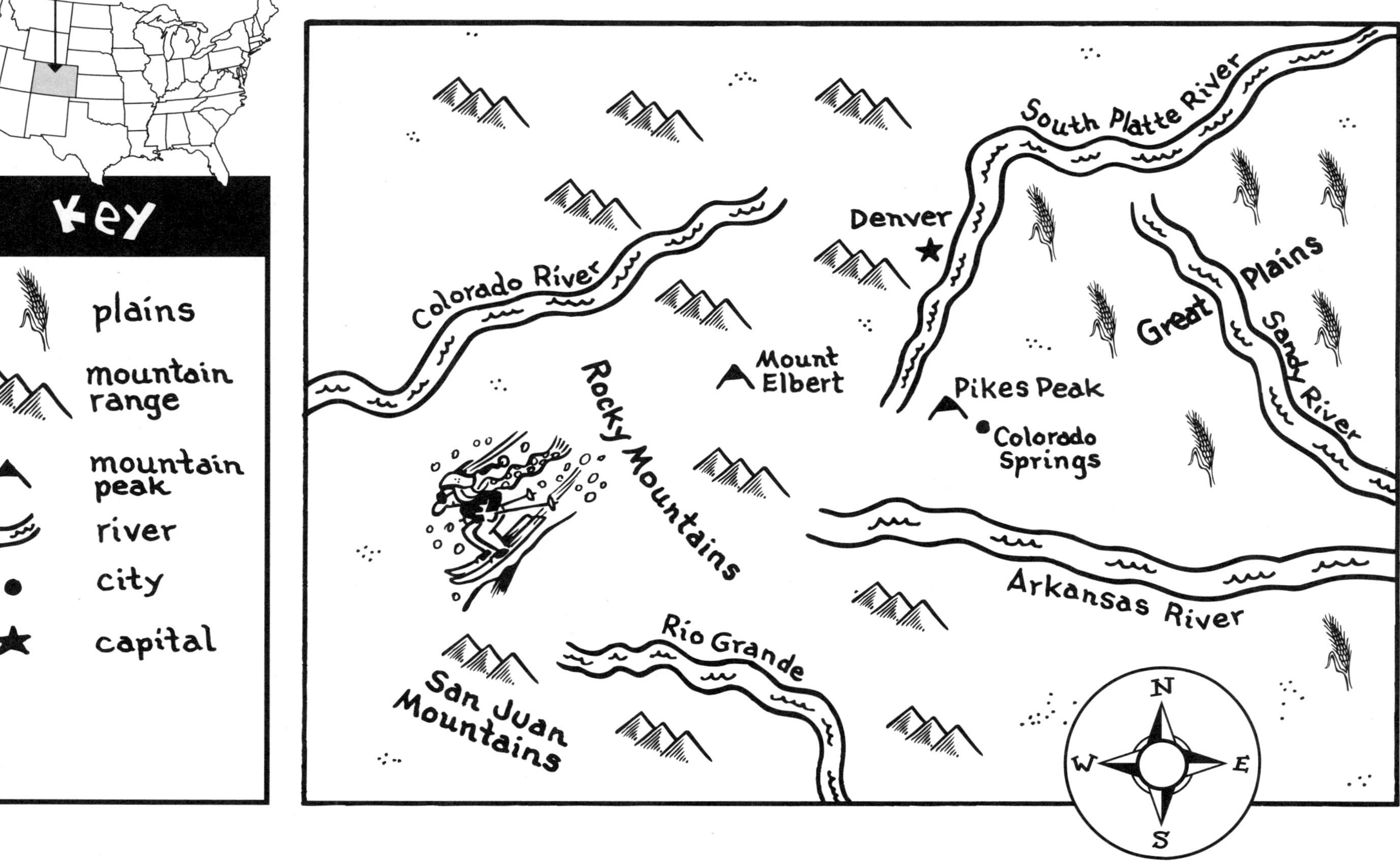

Key

plains

mountain range

mountain peak

river

city

capital

A Physical Map: Arizona

Arizona is known as the "Grand Canyon State." The Grand Canyon is 277 miles (446 km) long. It is 15 miles (24 km) wide. The canyon is more than a mile (1.6 km) deep. The Colorado River runs along the base of the canyon.

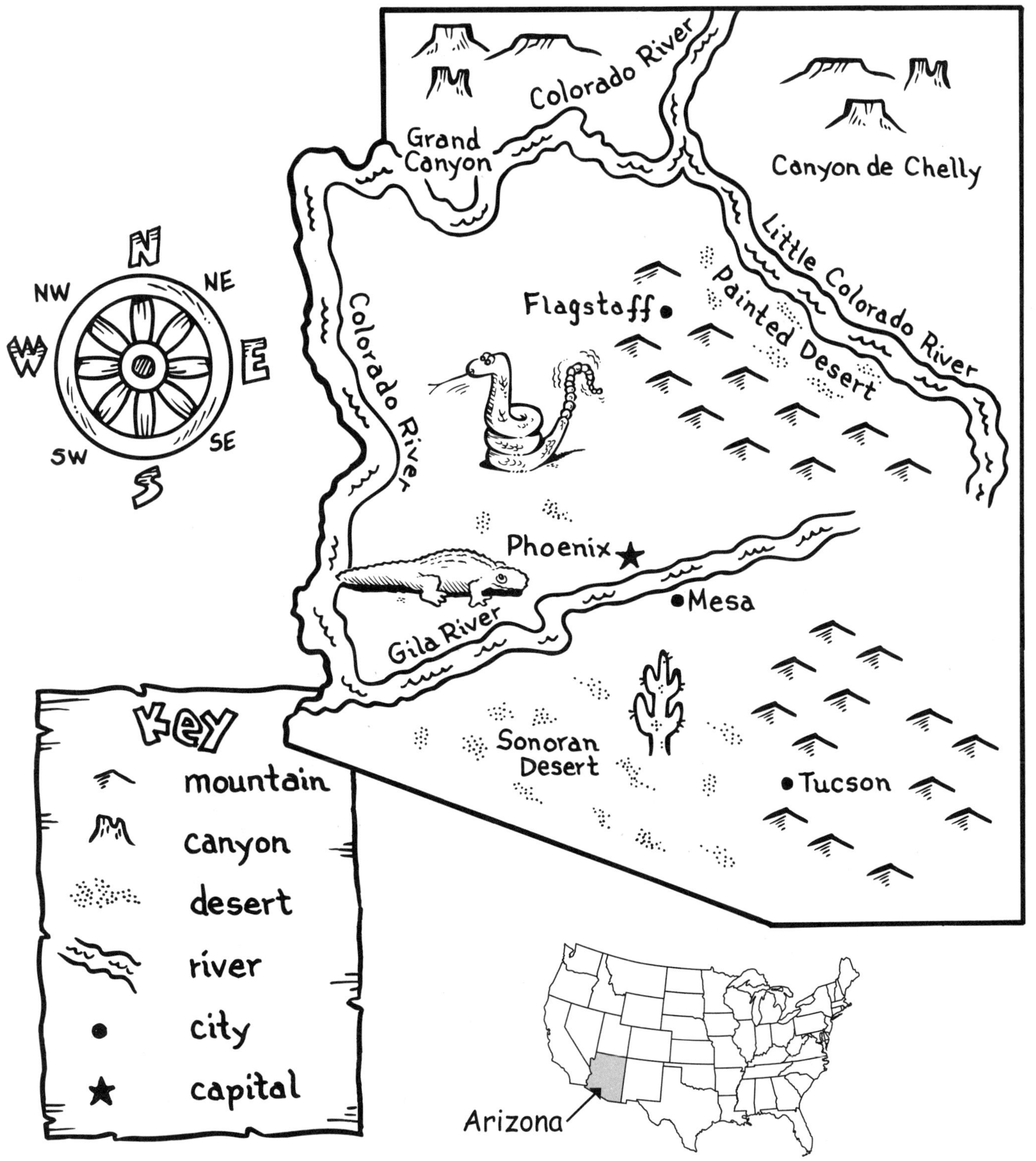

A Physical Map: Minnesota

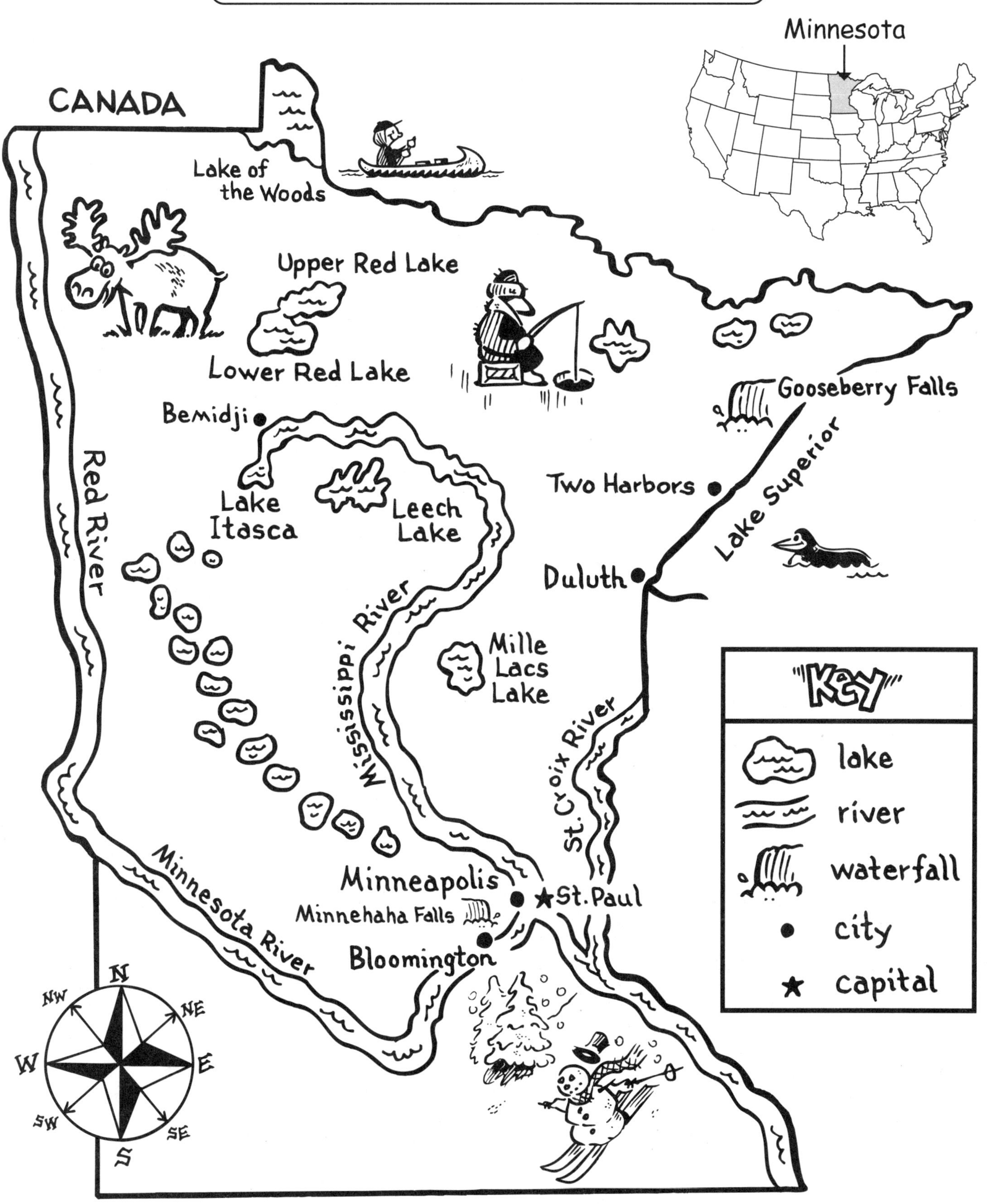

Minnesota is known as the "Land of 10,000 Lakes."

A Physical Map: Massachusetts

Massachusetts has a rugged coastline. Ships anchor in the safe harbors along the bays.

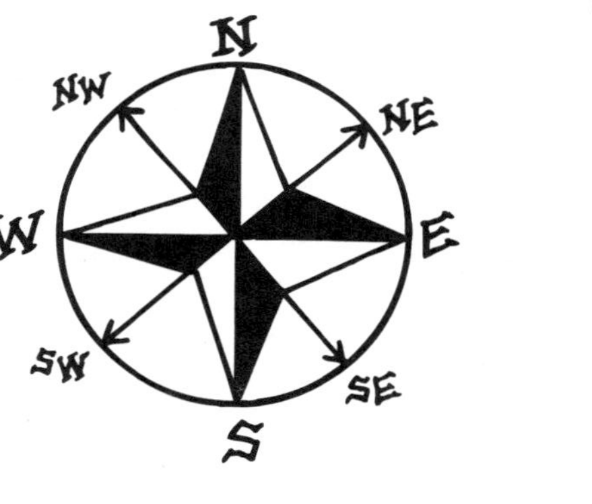

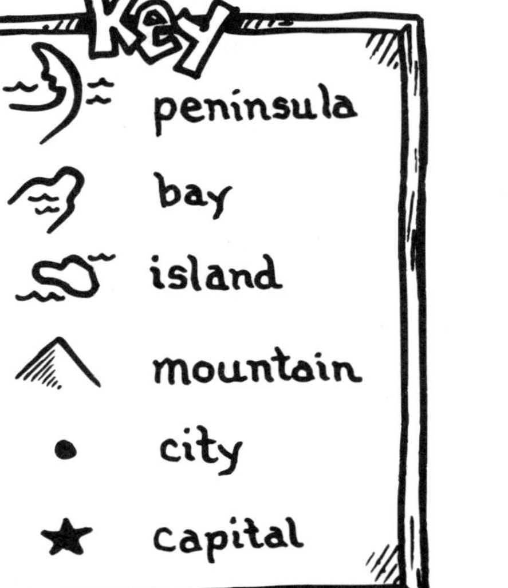

A Physical Map: Hawaii

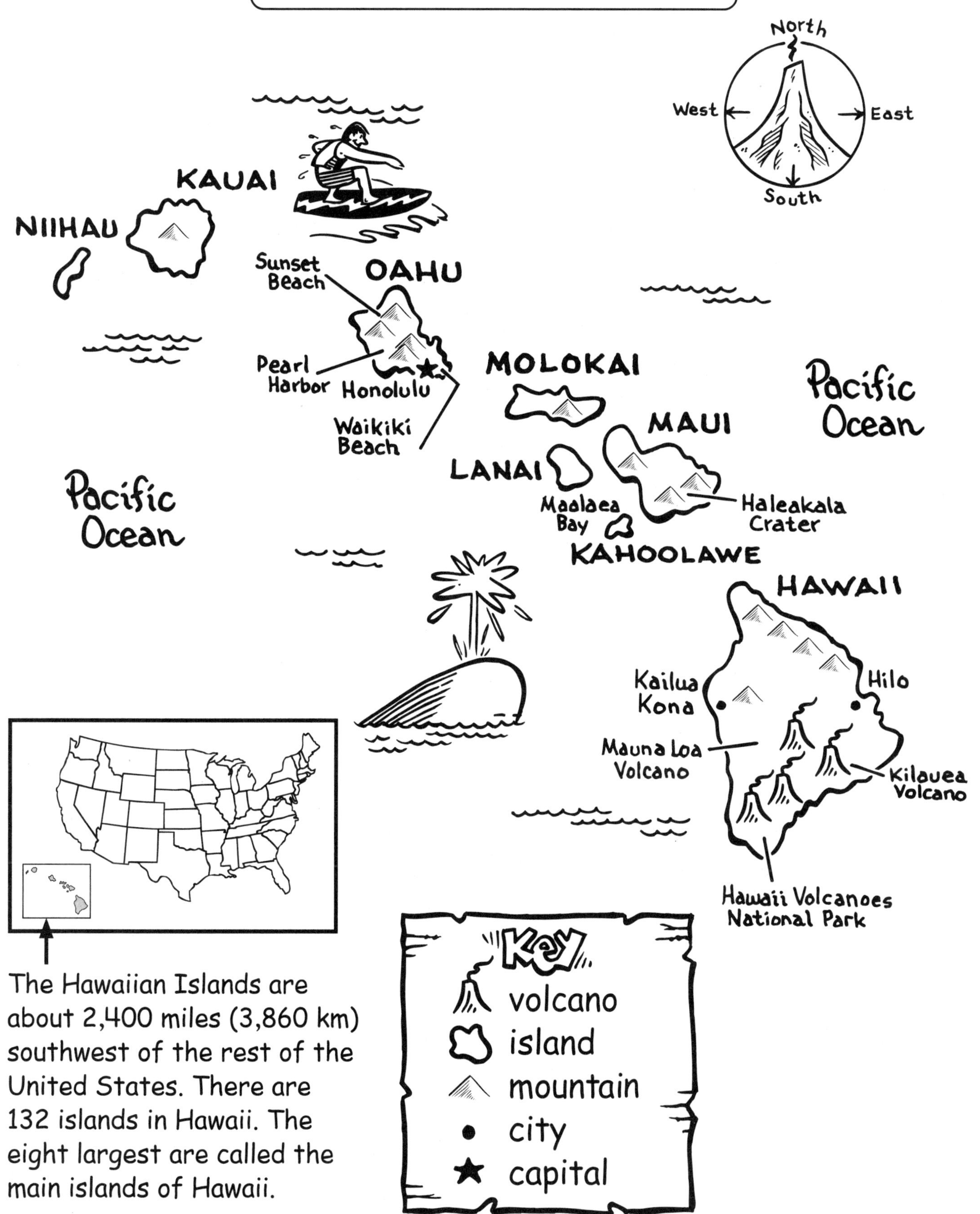

The Hawaiian Islands are about 2,400 miles (3,860 km) southwest of the rest of the United States. There are 132 islands in Hawaii. The eight largest are called the main islands of Hawaii.

The Pacific Region of the United States

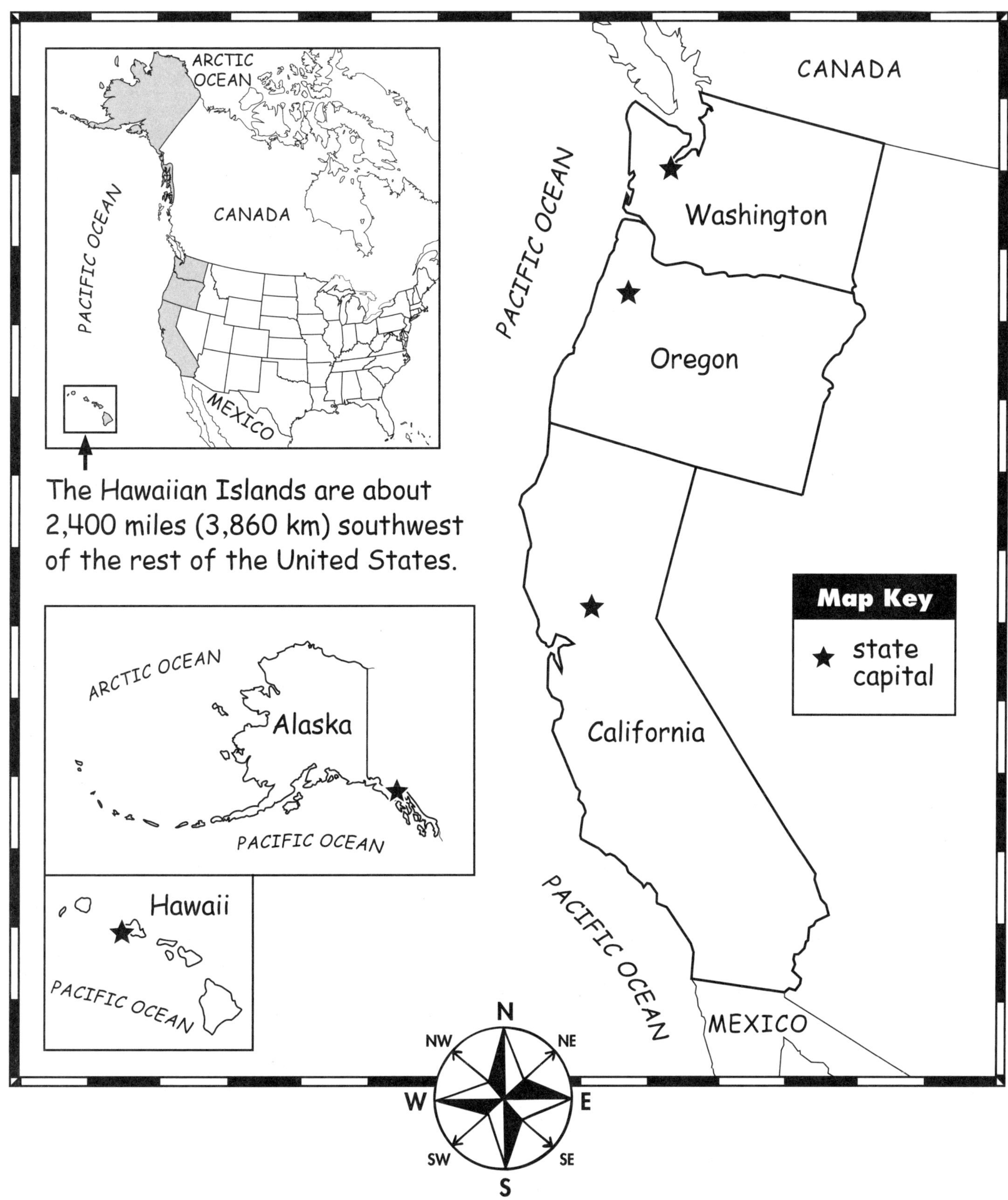

The Southwest Region of the United States

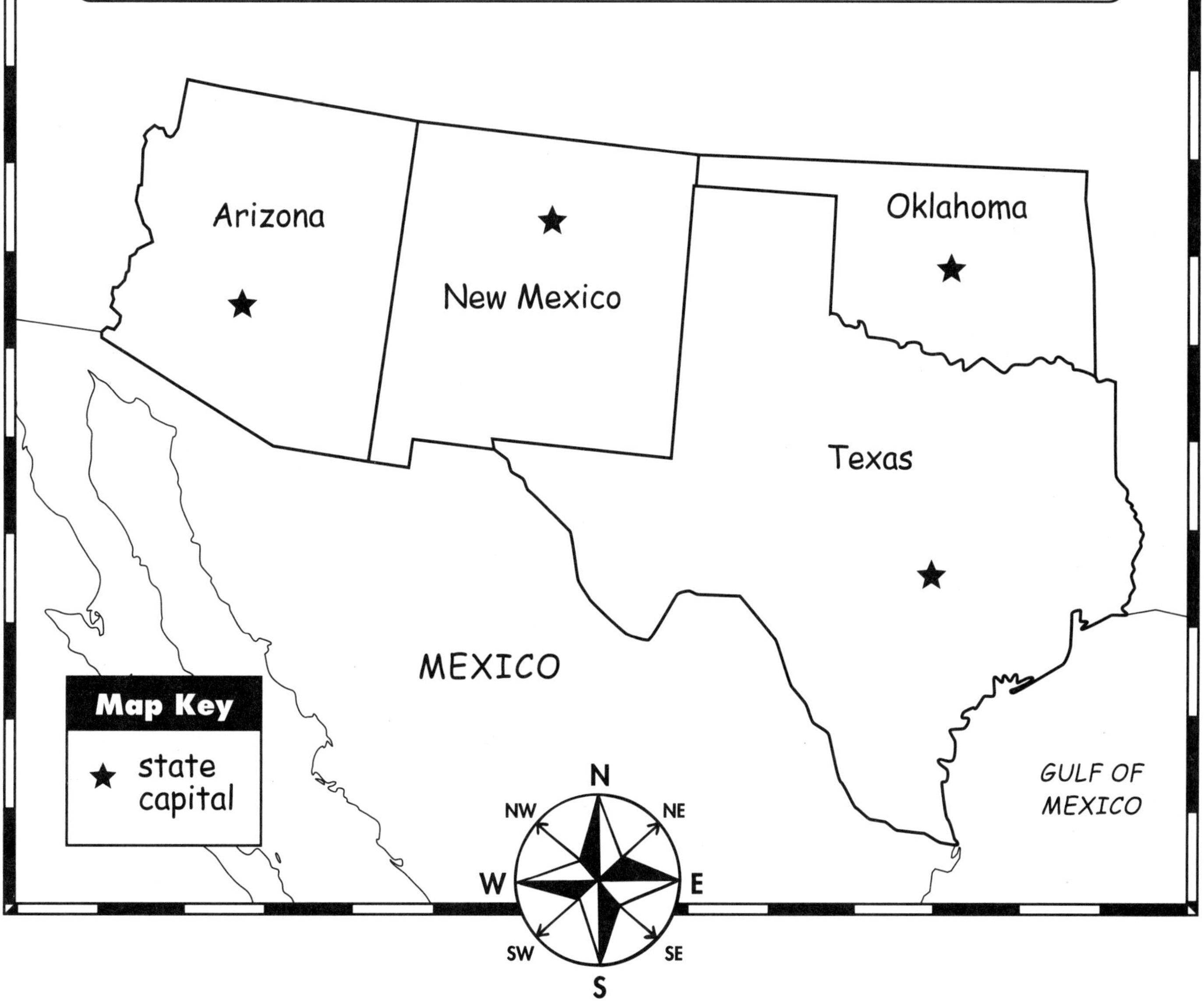

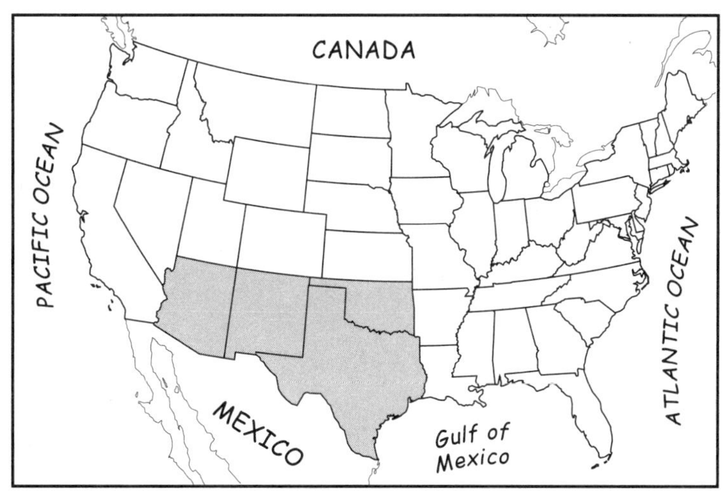

The Northeast Region of the United States

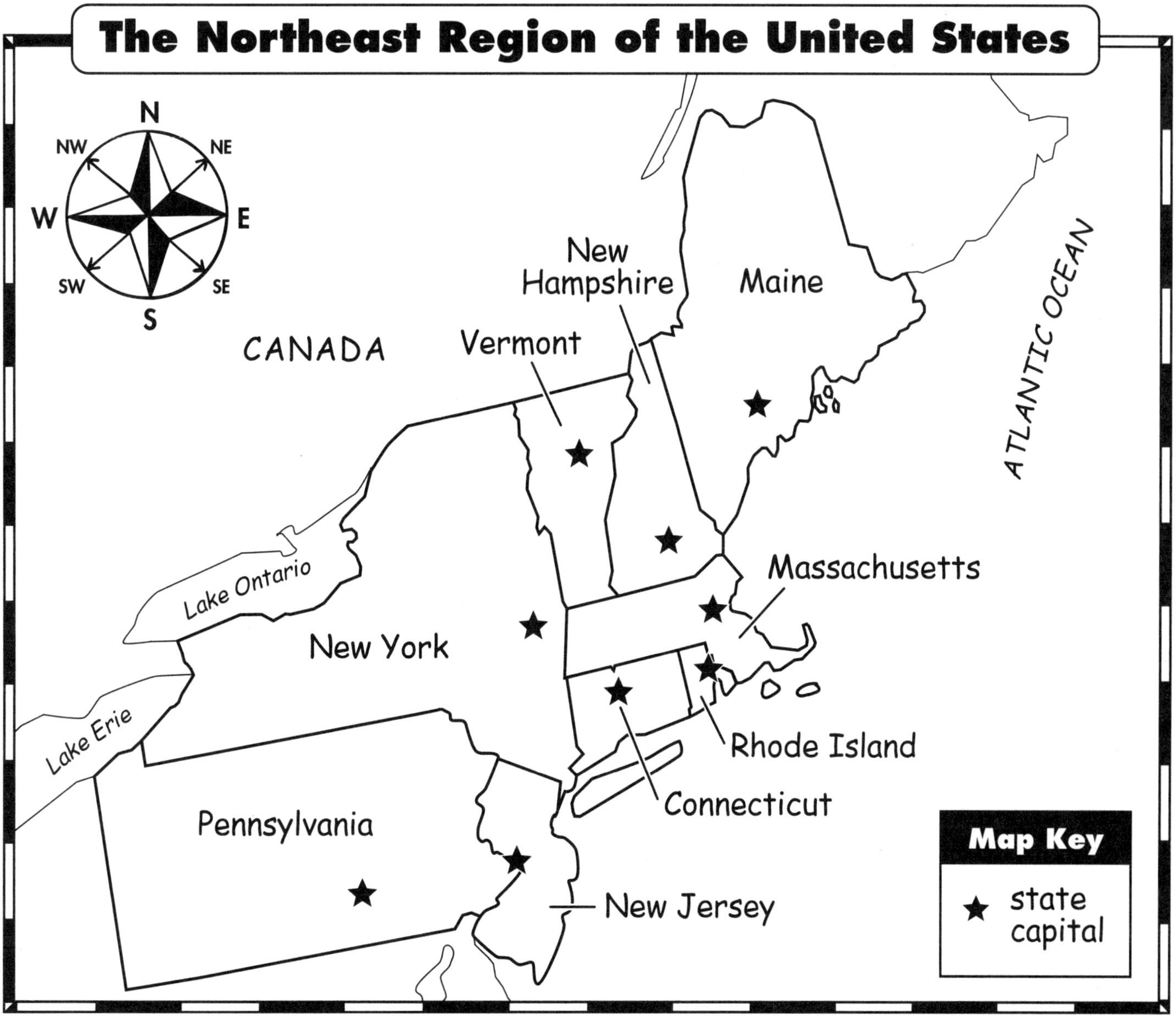

The Southeast Region of the United States

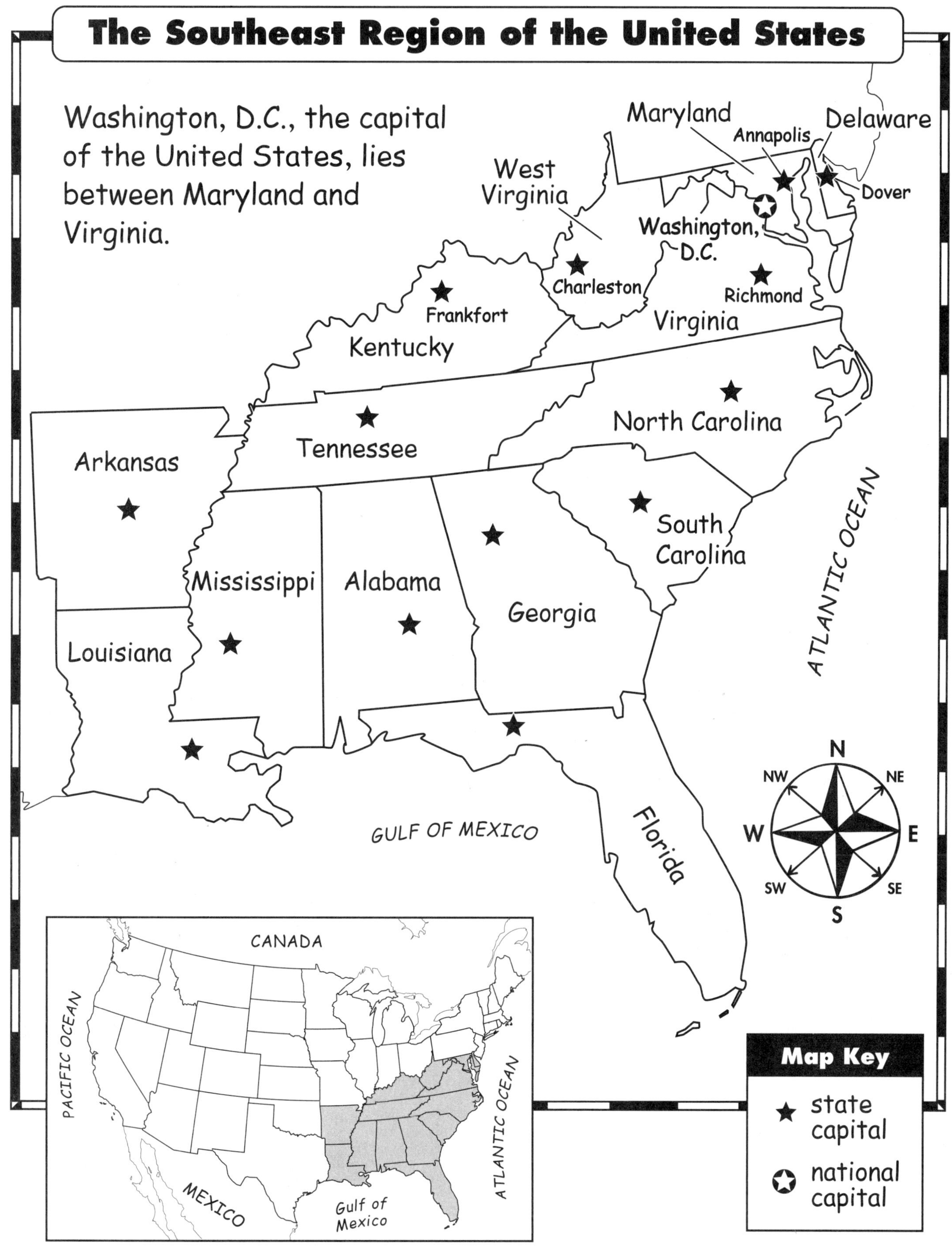

The Statue of Liberty

The Statue of Liberty stands on Liberty Island in New York Harbor. The copper monument is 151 feet (46 meters) tall. She stands on a concrete and stone base. The base is 154 feet (47 meters) high. Lady Liberty welcomes people to America. She stands for liberty, which means FREEDOM!

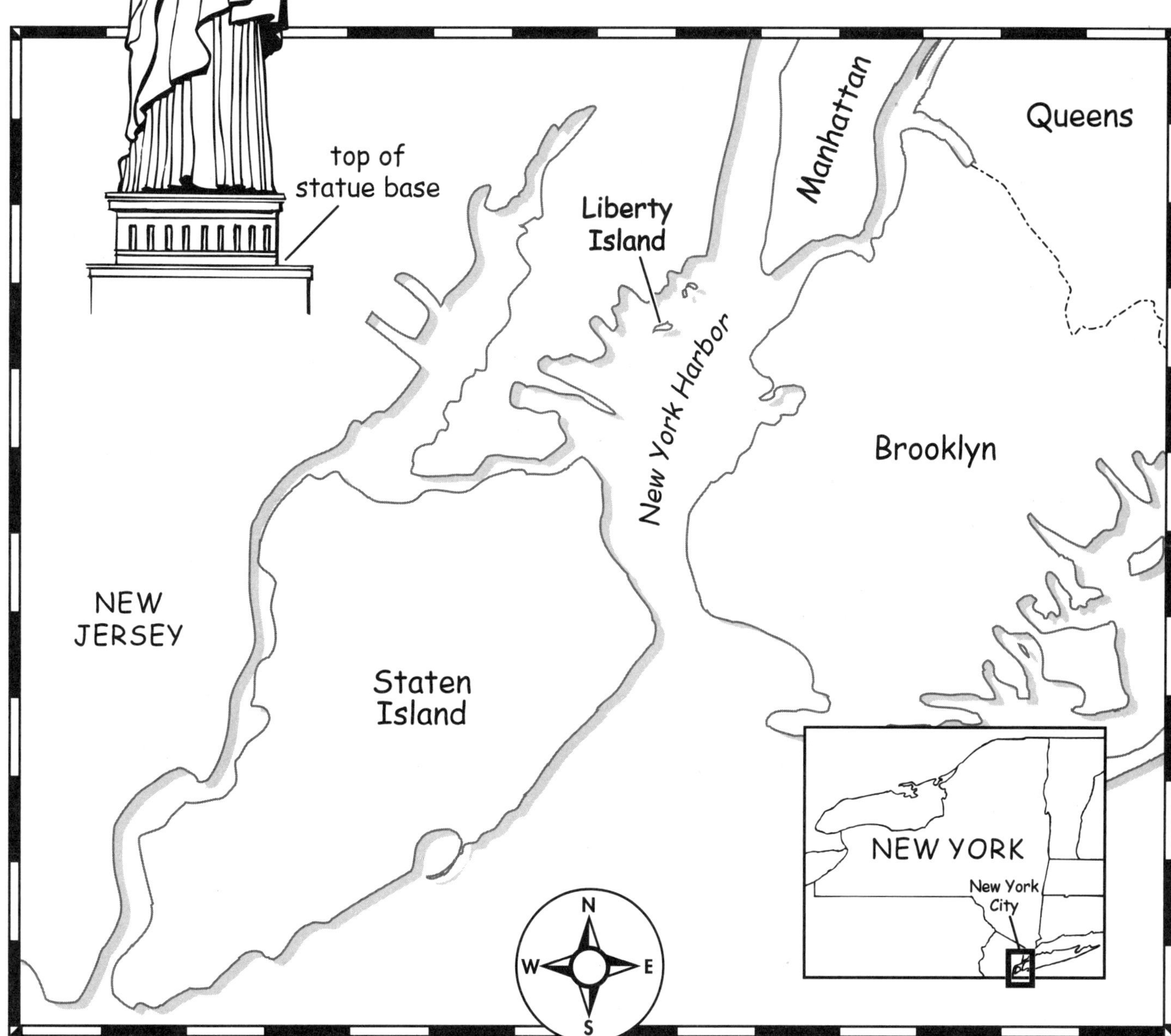

The White House

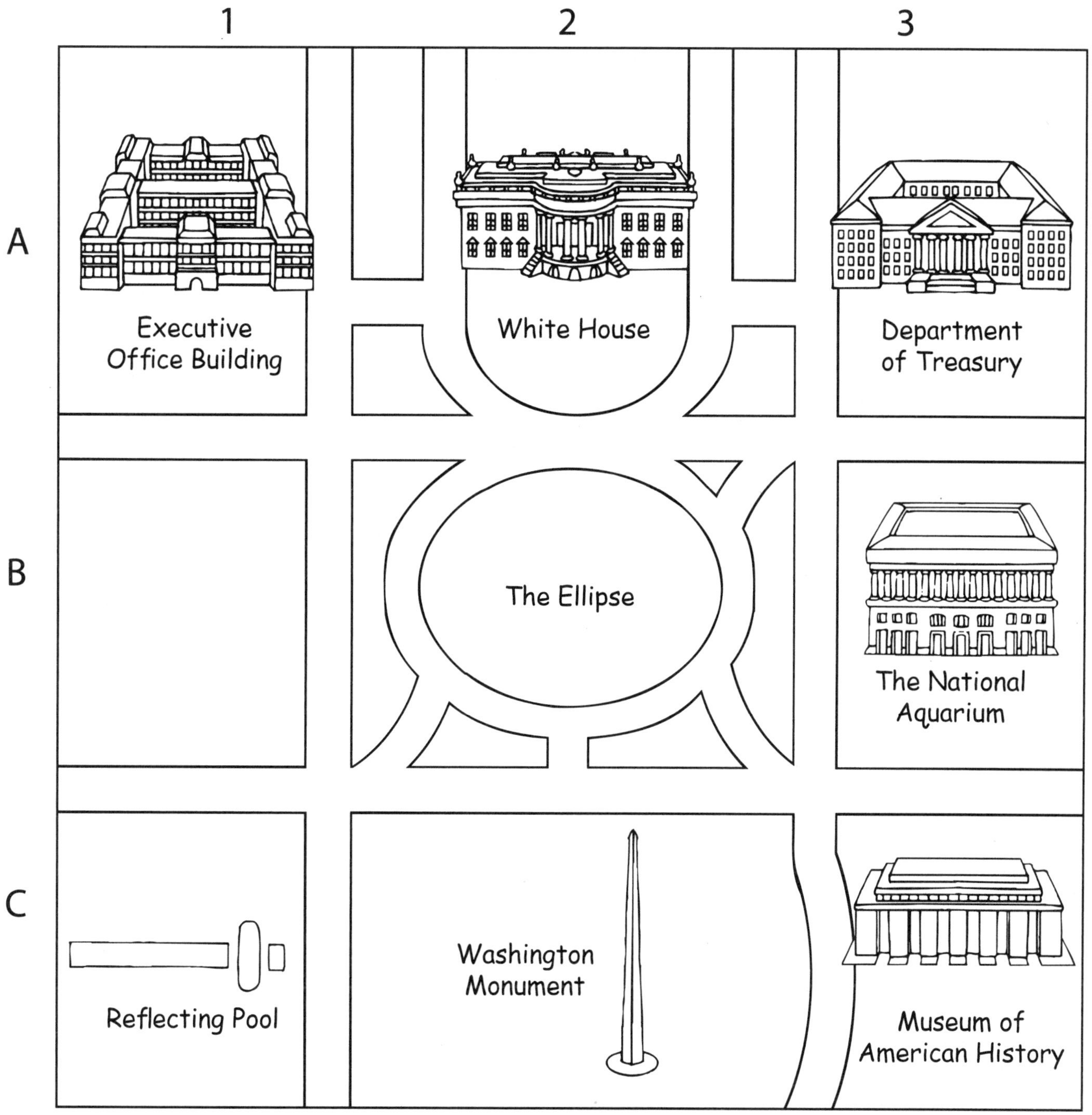

<table>
<tr><td></td><td>1</td><td>2</td><td>3</td></tr>
<tr><td>A</td><td>Executive Office Building</td><td>White House</td><td>Department of Treasury</td></tr>
<tr><td>B</td><td></td><td>The Ellipse</td><td>The National Aquarium</td></tr>
<tr><td>C</td><td>Reflecting Pool</td><td>Washington Monument</td><td>Museum of American History</td></tr>
</table>

- The president of the United States lives and works in the White House.

- The White House is located at 1600 Pennsylvania Avenue, Washington, D.C. 20500

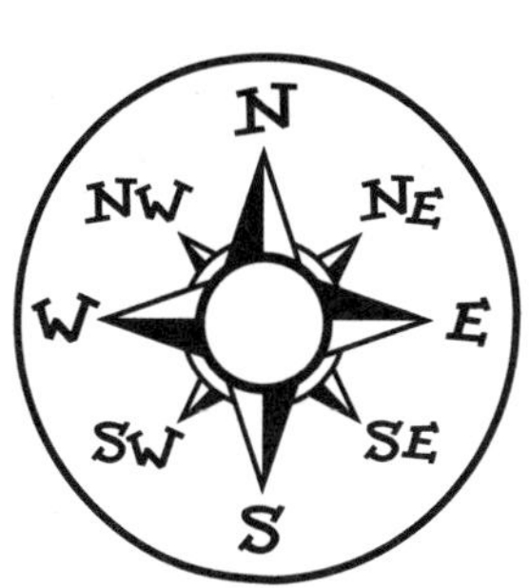

A Weather Map

The North-Central Region of the United States

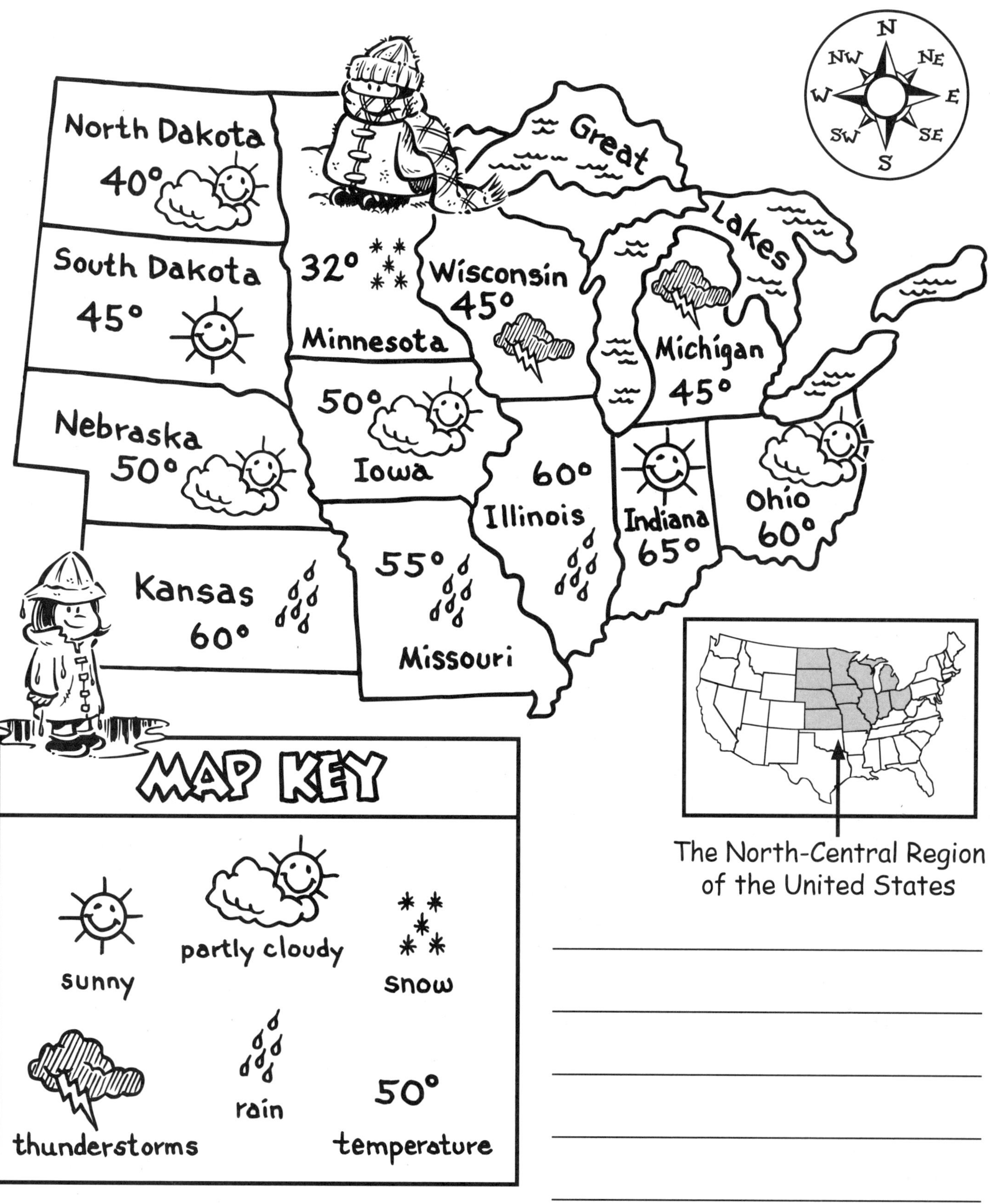

The North-Central Region
of the United States

Oregon's Forests

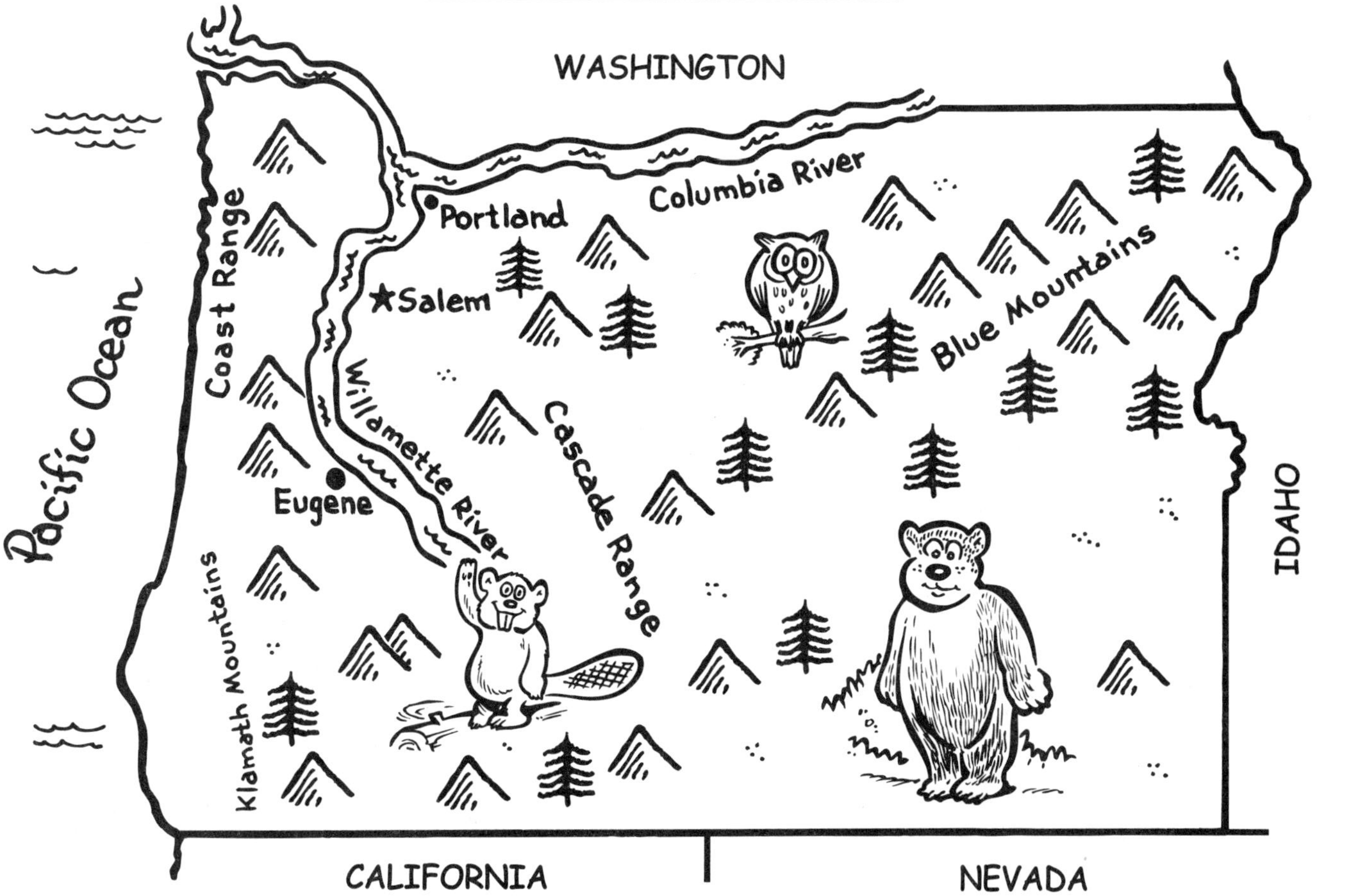

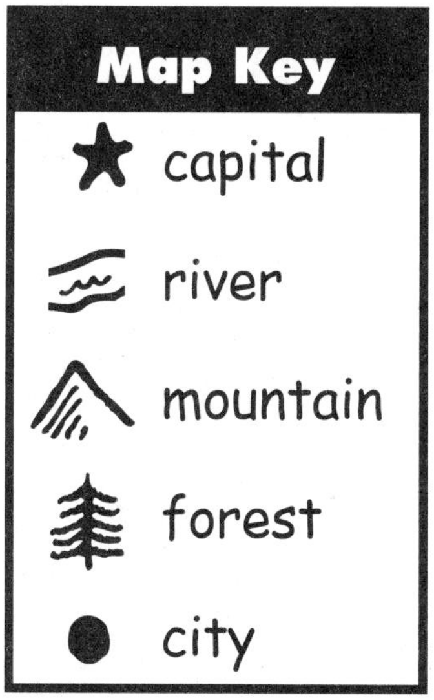

Map Key

- ★ capital
- river
- ⋀ mountain
- 🌲 forest
- ● city

Forest Animals

- black bear
- beaver
- black-tailed deer
- elk
- fox
- owl
- woodpecker

Forest Plants

- cedar tree
- fir tree
- pine tree
- spruce tree
- azalea
- laurel

- Nearly half of Oregon is covered with forests.

- There are eleven national forests in Oregon.

- The state tree of Oregon is the Douglas fir.

Ten Largest Cities in Wyoming

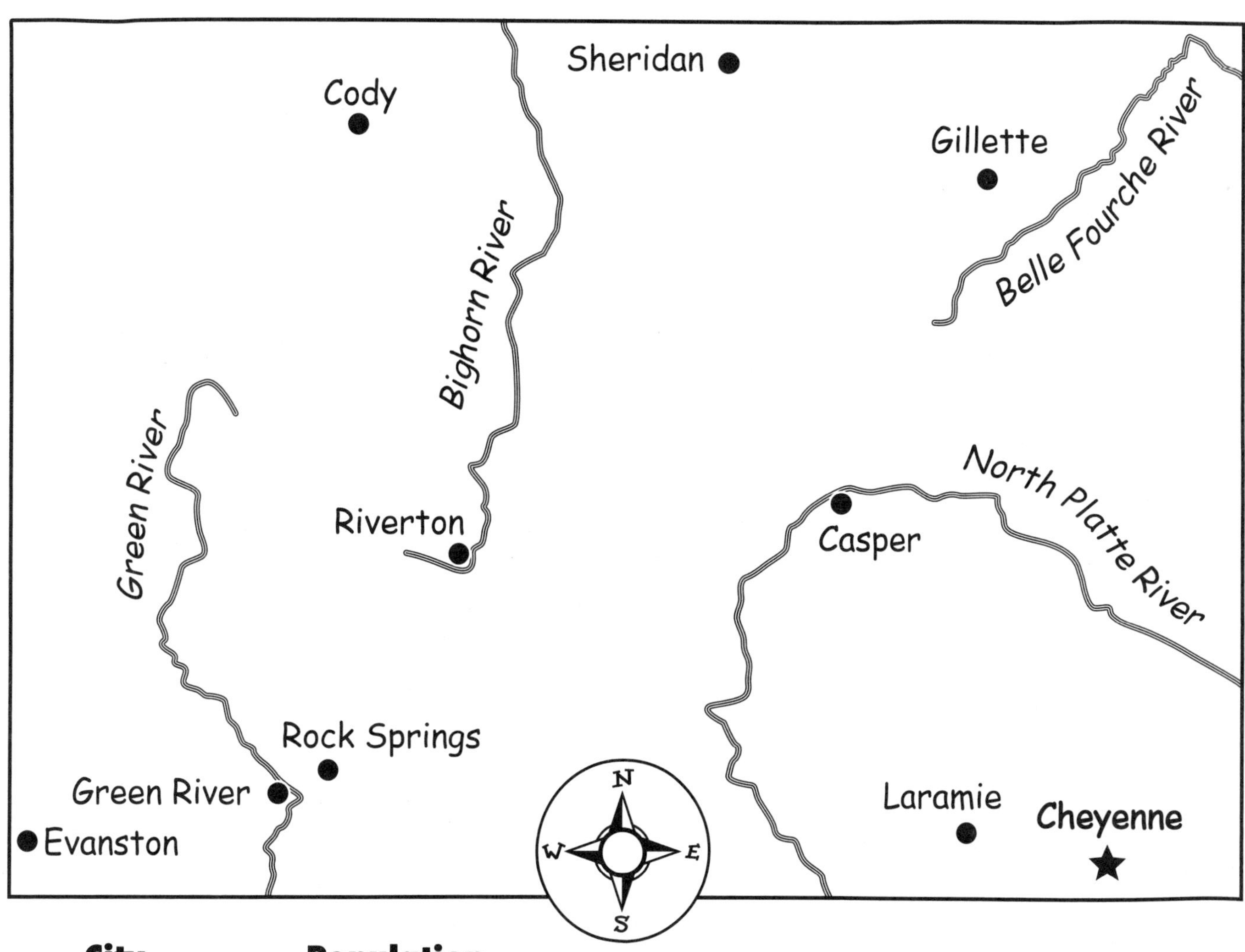

City	Population
Casper	55,316
Cheyenne	59,466
Cody	9,520
Evanston	12,359
Gillette	29,087
Green River	12,515
Laramie	30,816
Riverton	10,615
Rock Springs	23,036
Sheridan	17,444

Population based on 2010 census

Key

★ state capital
● city
— state border
〜 river

Wyoming

A County Fair

A Product Map: Wisconsin

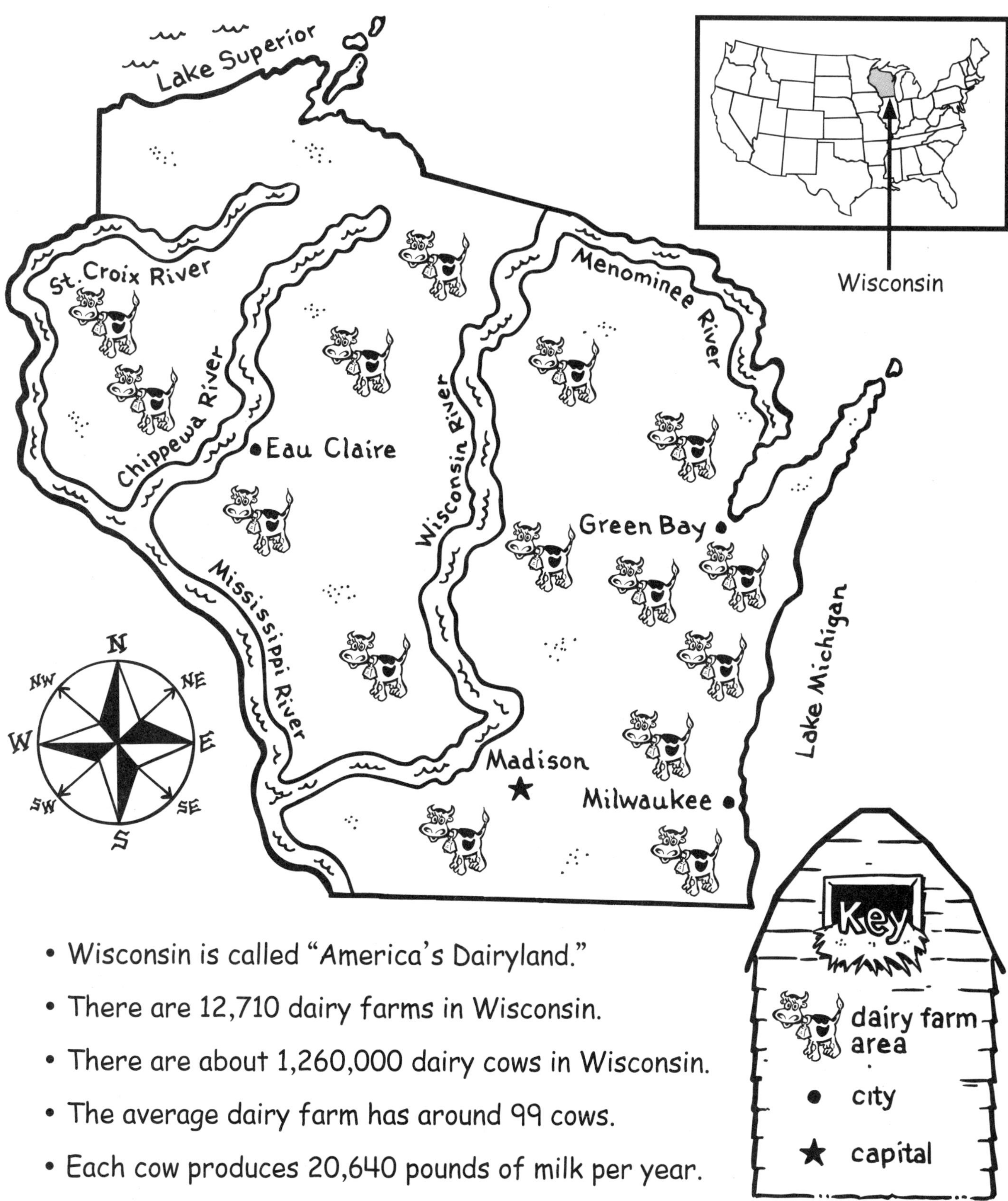

- Wisconsin is called "America's Dairyland."

- There are 12,710 dairy farms in Wisconsin.

- There are about 1,260,000 dairy cows in Wisconsin.

- The average dairy farm has around 99 cows.

- Each cow produces 20,640 pounds of milk per year.

- It takes about 10 pounds of milk to make 1 pound of cheese.

- It takes about 21 pounds of milk to make 1 pound of butter.

Living in a Community

First Street

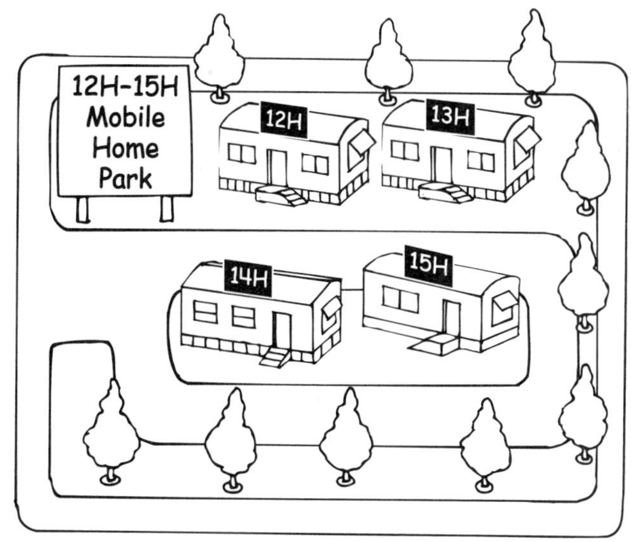

Community Services

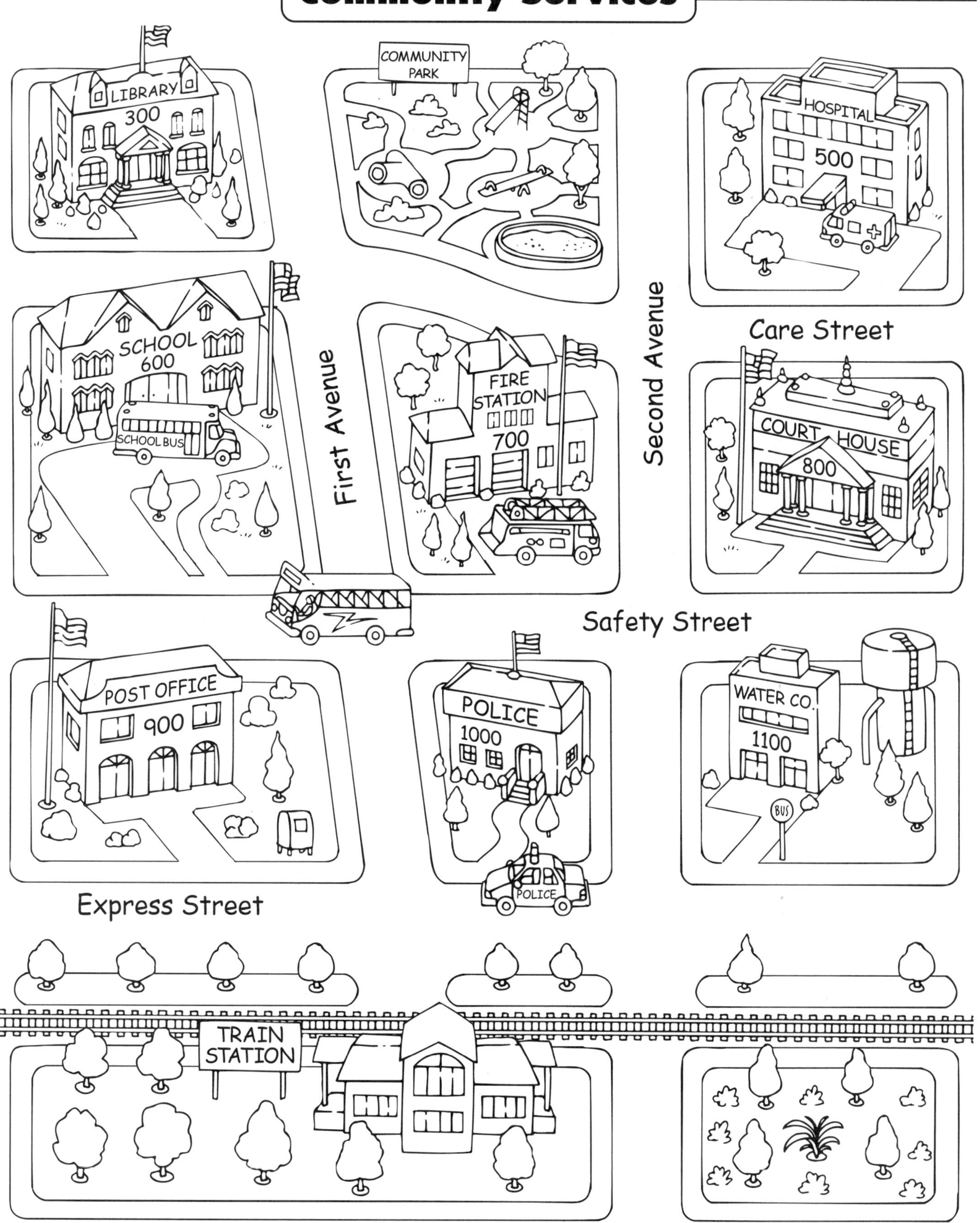

A community provides services for its people.

The Bluegrass Region of Kentucky

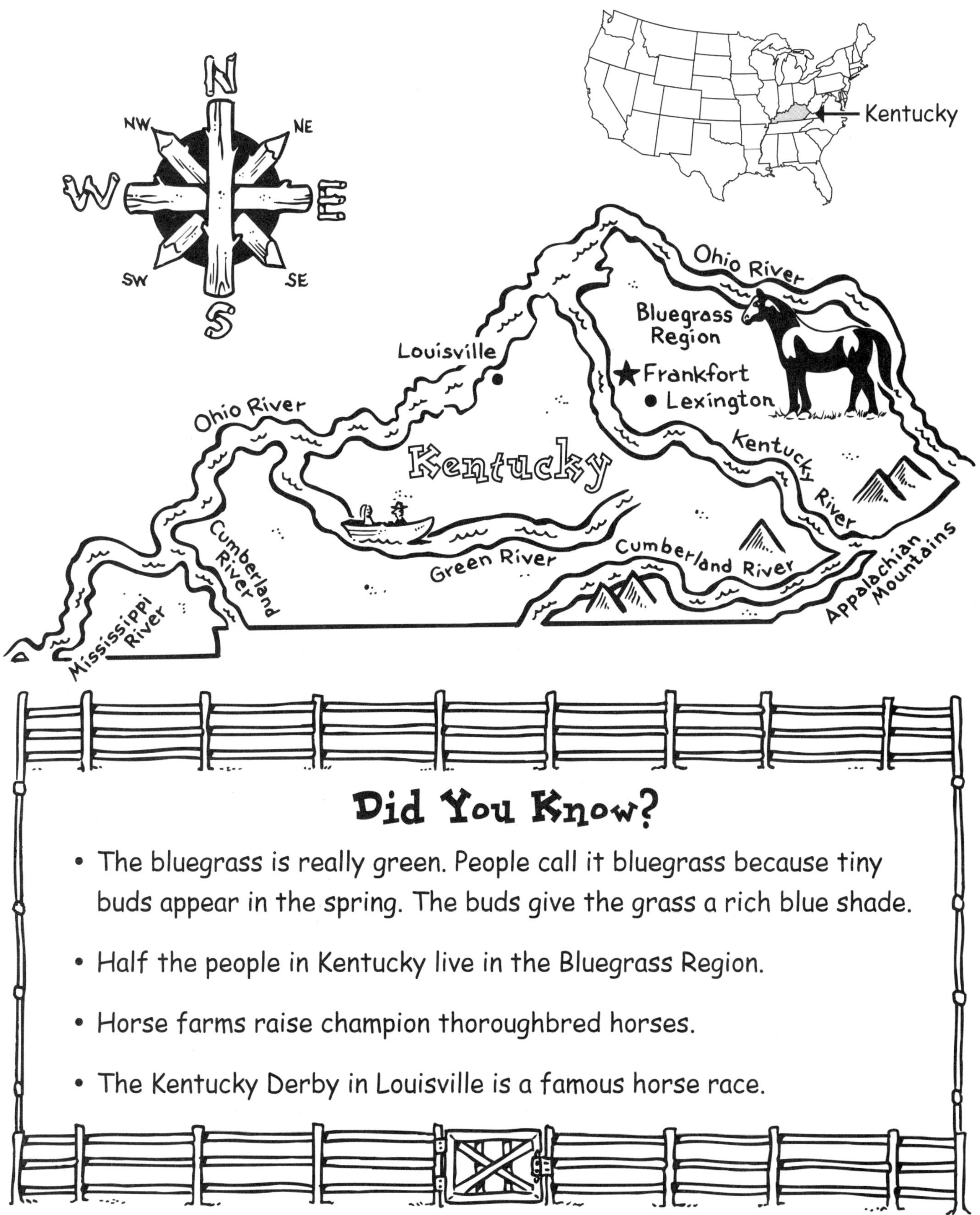

Did You Know?

- The bluegrass is really green. People call it bluegrass because tiny buds appear in the spring. The buds give the grass a rich blue shade.

- Half the people in Kentucky live in the Bluegrass Region.

- Horse farms raise champion thoroughbred horses.

- The Kentucky Derby in Louisville is a famous horse race.

A Tourist Map

California

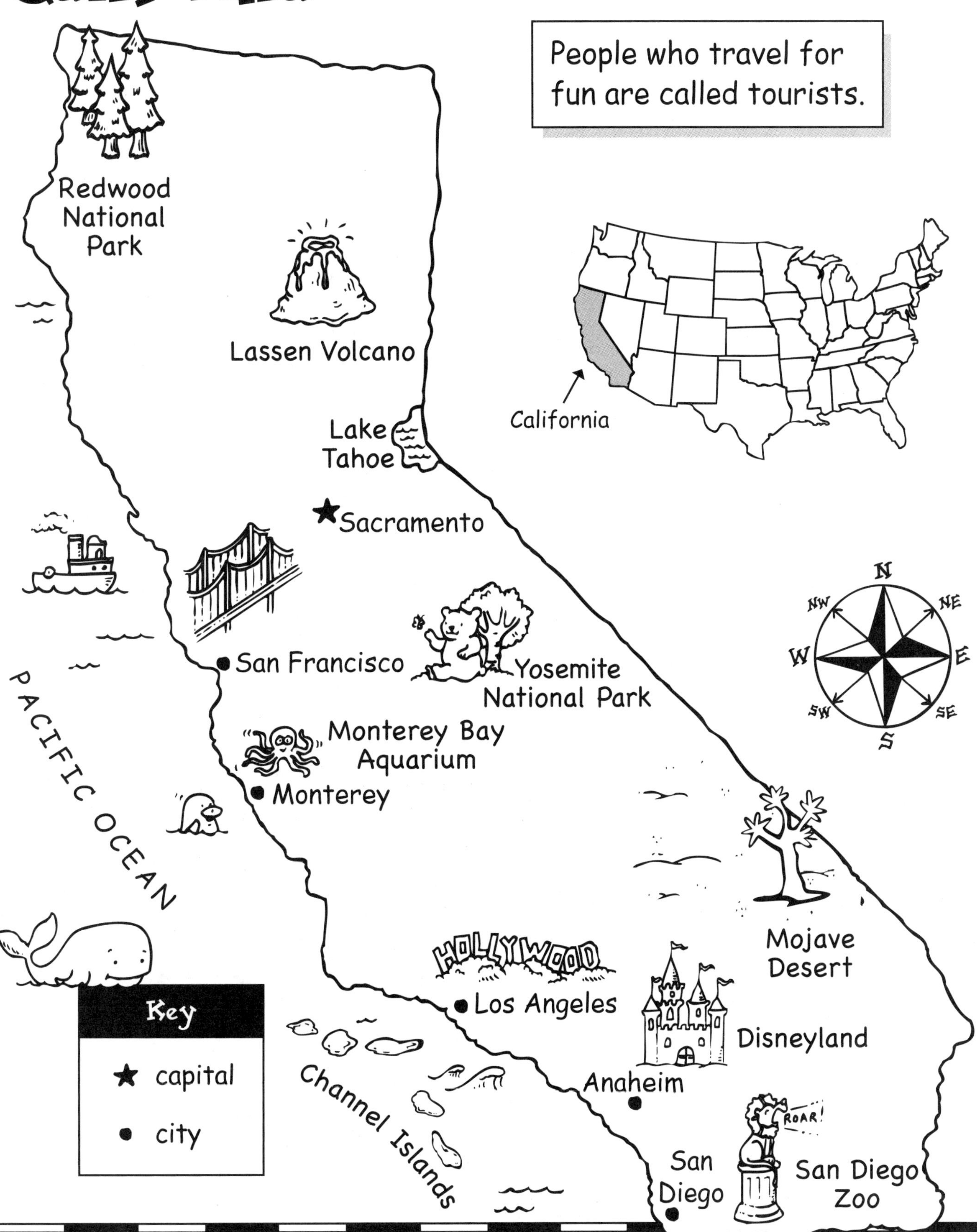

Minerals of Alaska

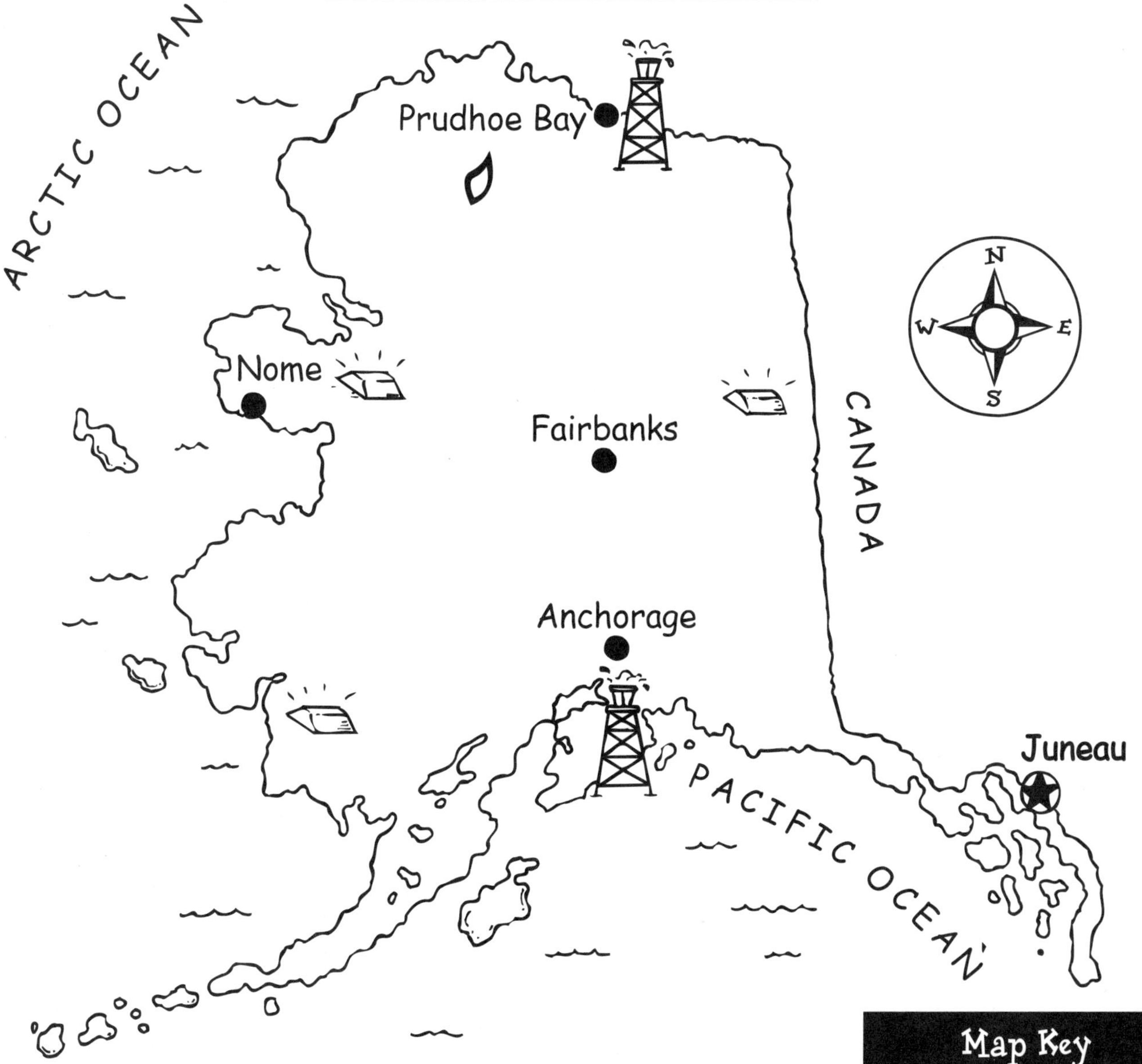

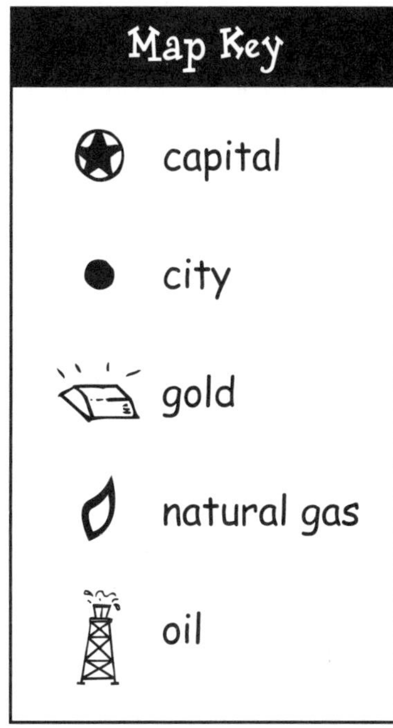

Map labels: ARCTIC OCEAN · Prudhoe Bay · Nome · Fairbanks · CANADA · Anchorage · Juneau · PACIFIC OCEAN

Did You Know?

- Oil, natural gas, and gold are three minerals produced in Alaska.

- Alaska's oil wells produce almost 1 million barrels of oil every day.

- Natural gas comes from drilled wells, just like oil.

- Most of Alaska's gold deposits are found near Fairbanks and Nome.

The Lewis and Clark Trail

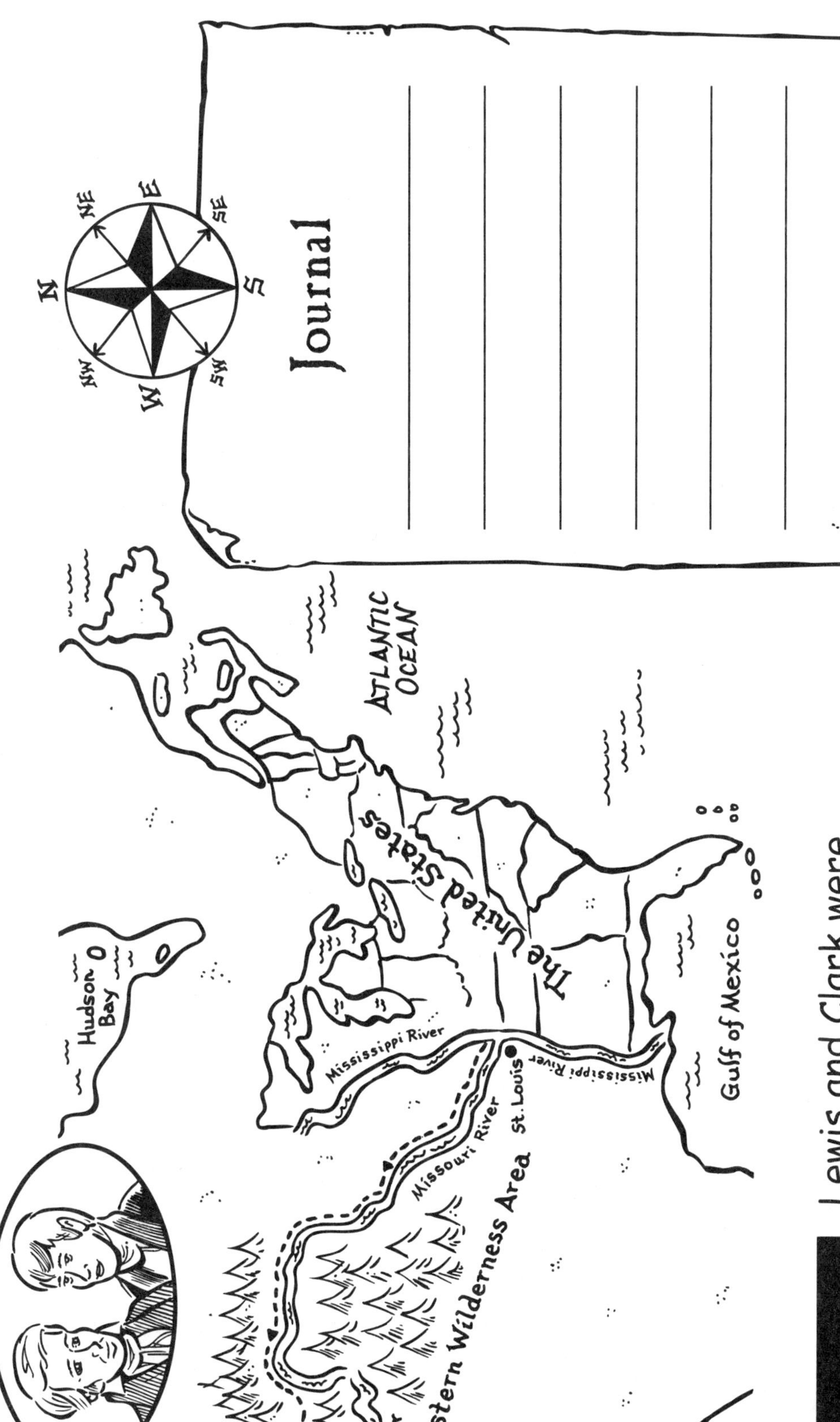

Lewis and Clark were explorers. They traveled 8,000 miles (12,800 km) across the western wilderness. They discovered new lands for the United States.

A Neighborhood Plan

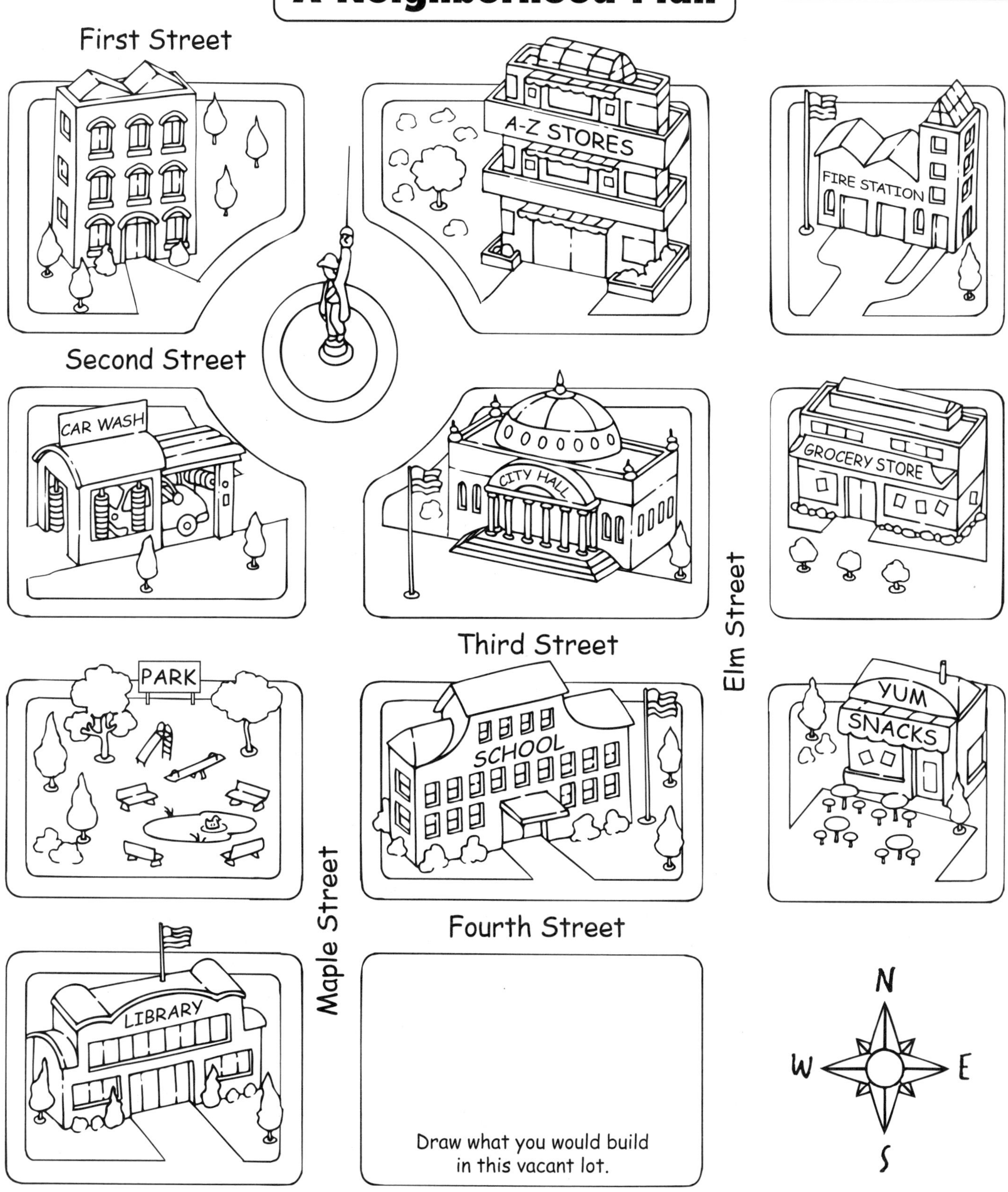

The map shows a neighborhood. There is a vacant lot.
What would you build there? Make a plan.

What Is a Globe?

Thursday

1. Is Australia south or north of the equator?

   ____

2. Is most of South America north or south of the equator?

   ____

Friday

1. On which continent do you live?

   ____

2. Do you live north or south of the equator?

   ____

Challenge

On all three globes, color the oceans blue.
Color the continents green.

   Daily Geography Practice • EMC 6853 • © Evan-Moor Corporation

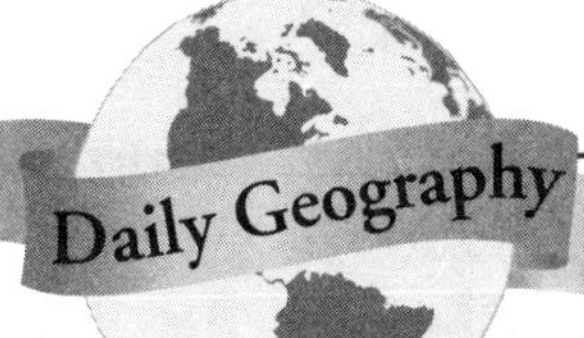

Parts of a Map

Thursday

1. How many avenues are on this map? What are their names?

____

2. Does Highway 68 run east and west, or north and south?

____

Friday

1. Is Night's Inn on the west or east end of Beach Road?

____

2. Which two businesses are east of Second Avenue?

____

Challenge

What would you call this small town? Write a new title for this map. Write the new title on the map.

   Daily Geography Practice • EMC 6853 • © Evan-Moor Corporation

A Map Grid and a Map Index

Thursday

1. Huntsville shares a square with which other city?

   ____

2. In which square is Decatur?

   ____

Friday

1. What is the capital of Alabama? In which two squares is it?

   ____

2. What does the map index show?

   ____

   ____

Challenge

On the map:

- Color square E2 red.
- Color square G4 green.

Daily Geography Practice • EMC 6853 • © Evan-Moor Corporation

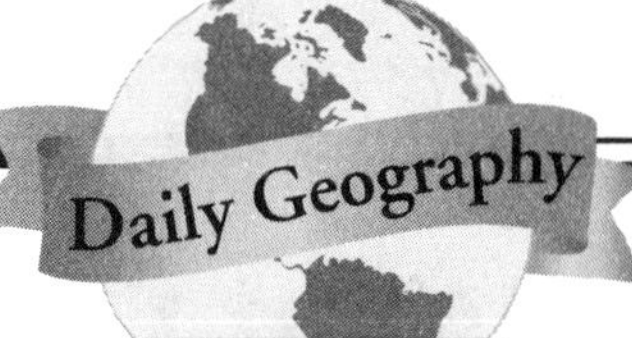

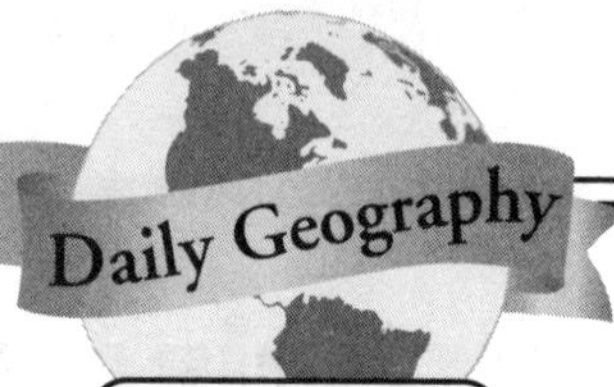

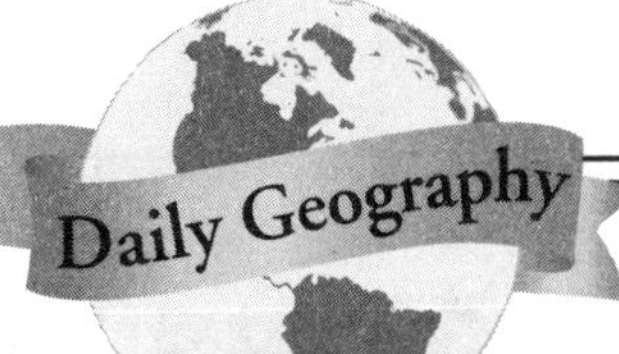

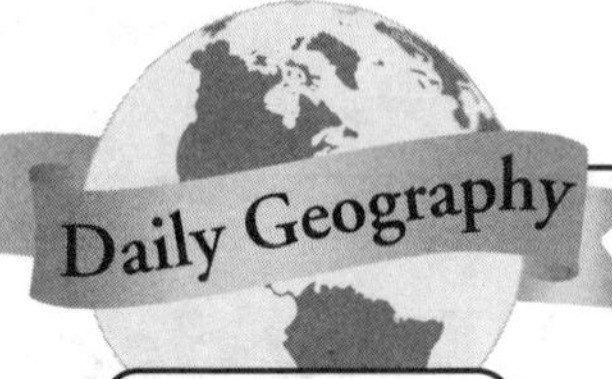

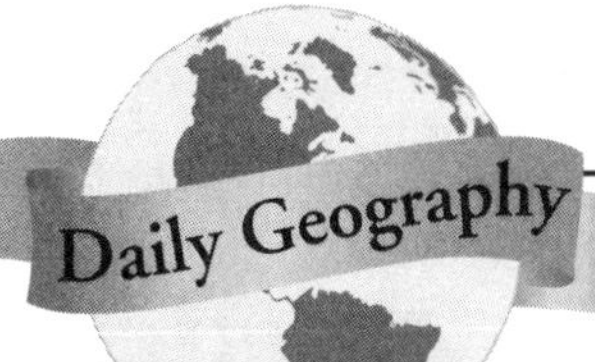

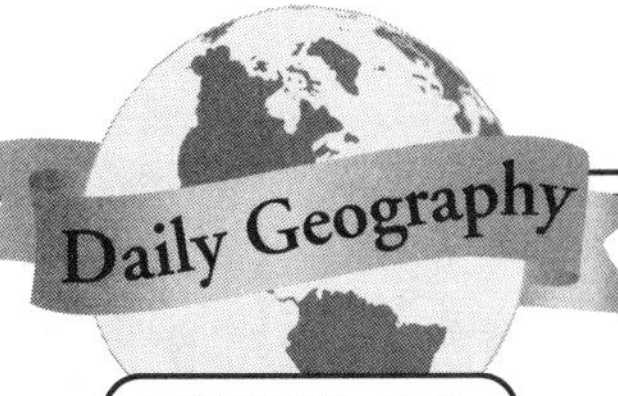

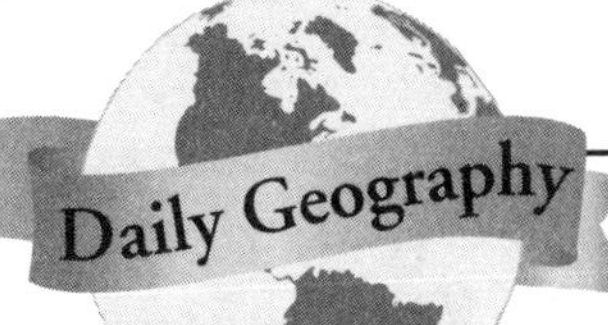

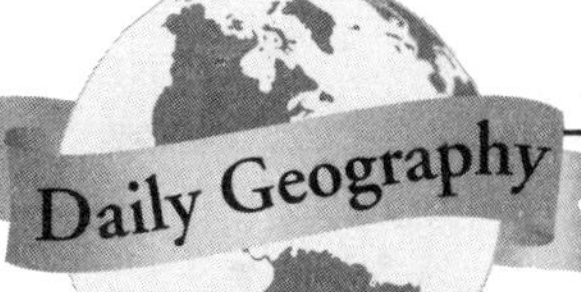

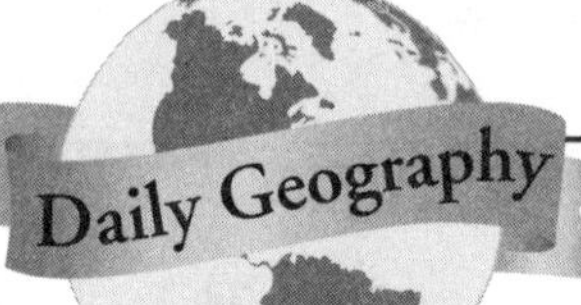

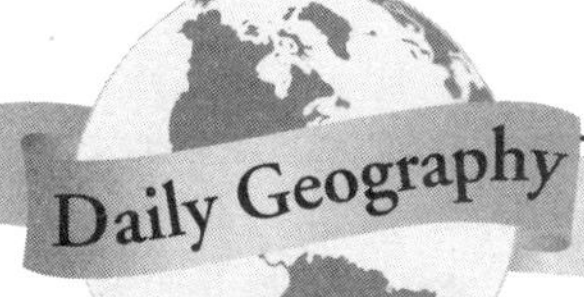

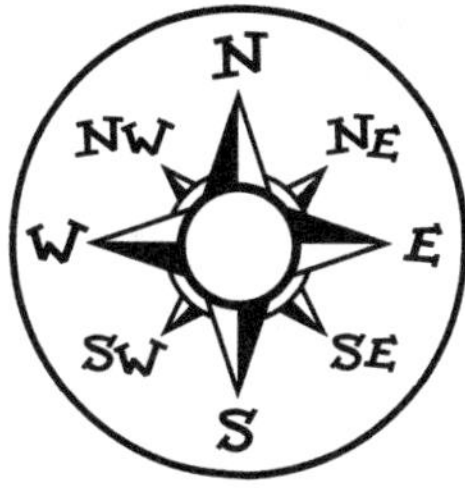

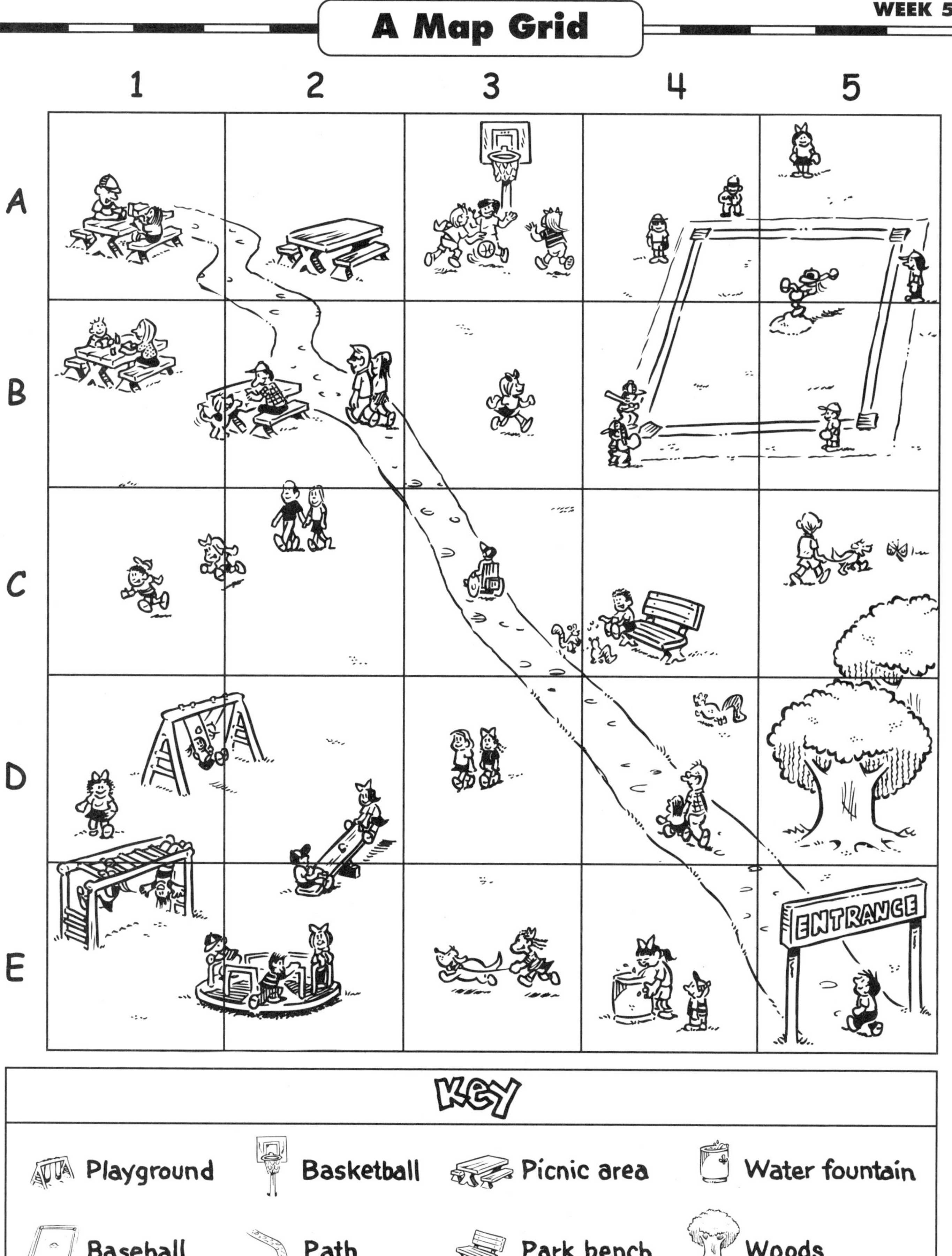

WEEK 5
A Map Grid
1 2 3 4 5
A
B
C
D
E
ENTRANCE
KEY
Playground
Basketball
Picnic area
Water fountain
Baseball
Path
Park bench
Woods

A Map Grid and a Map Index

Alabama

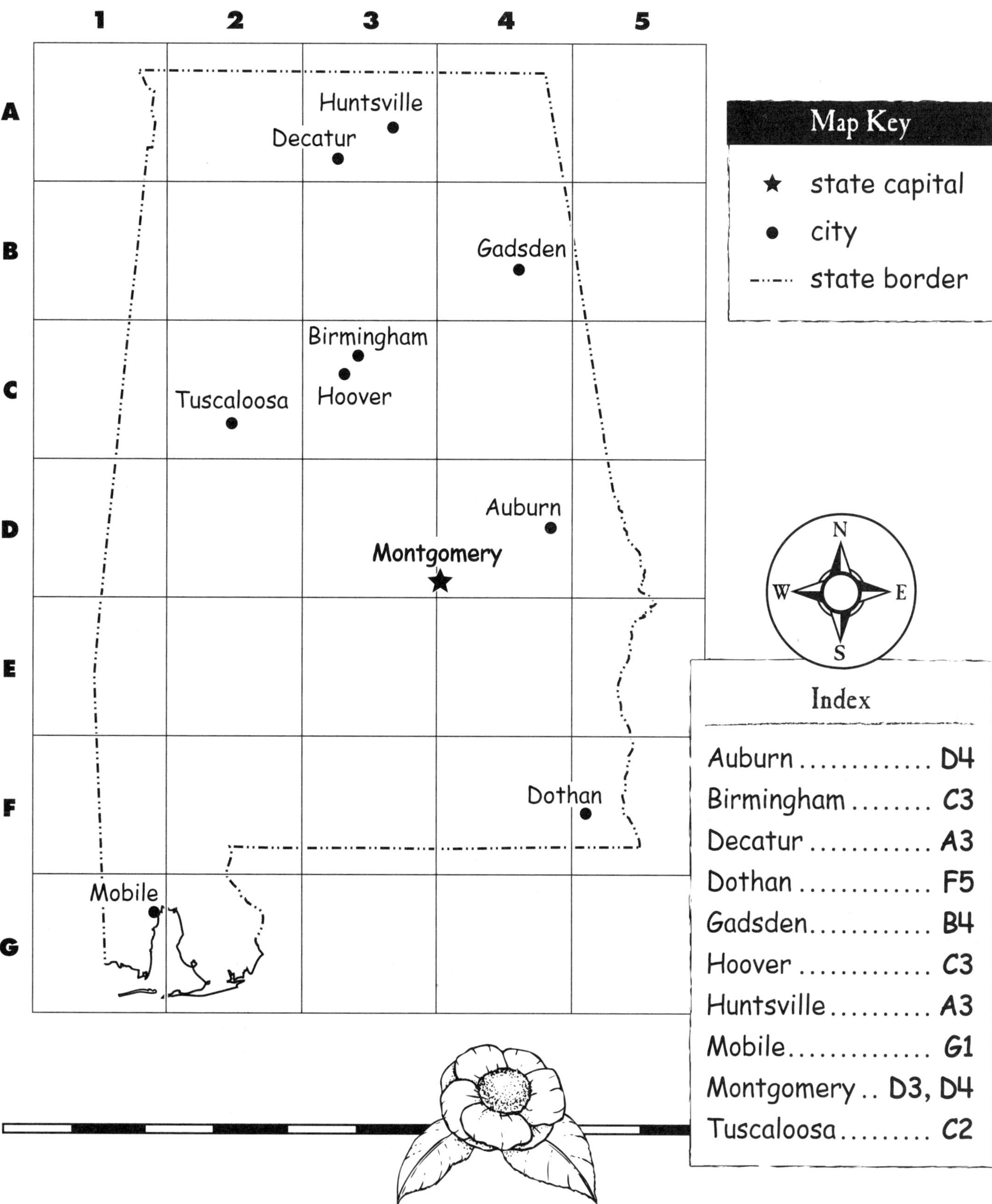

A Map Scale

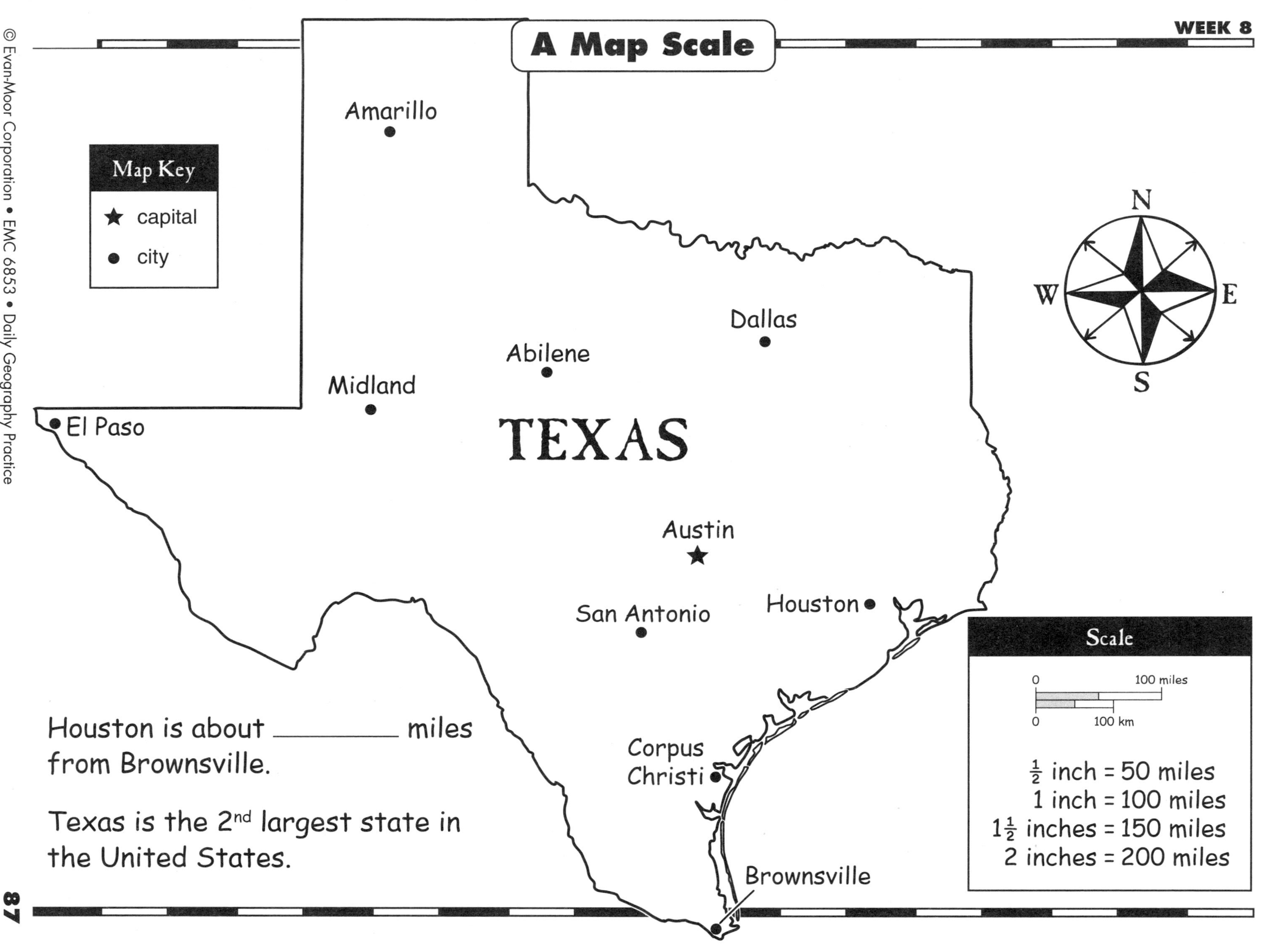

Houston is about _______ miles from Brownsville.

Texas is the 2nd largest state in the United States.

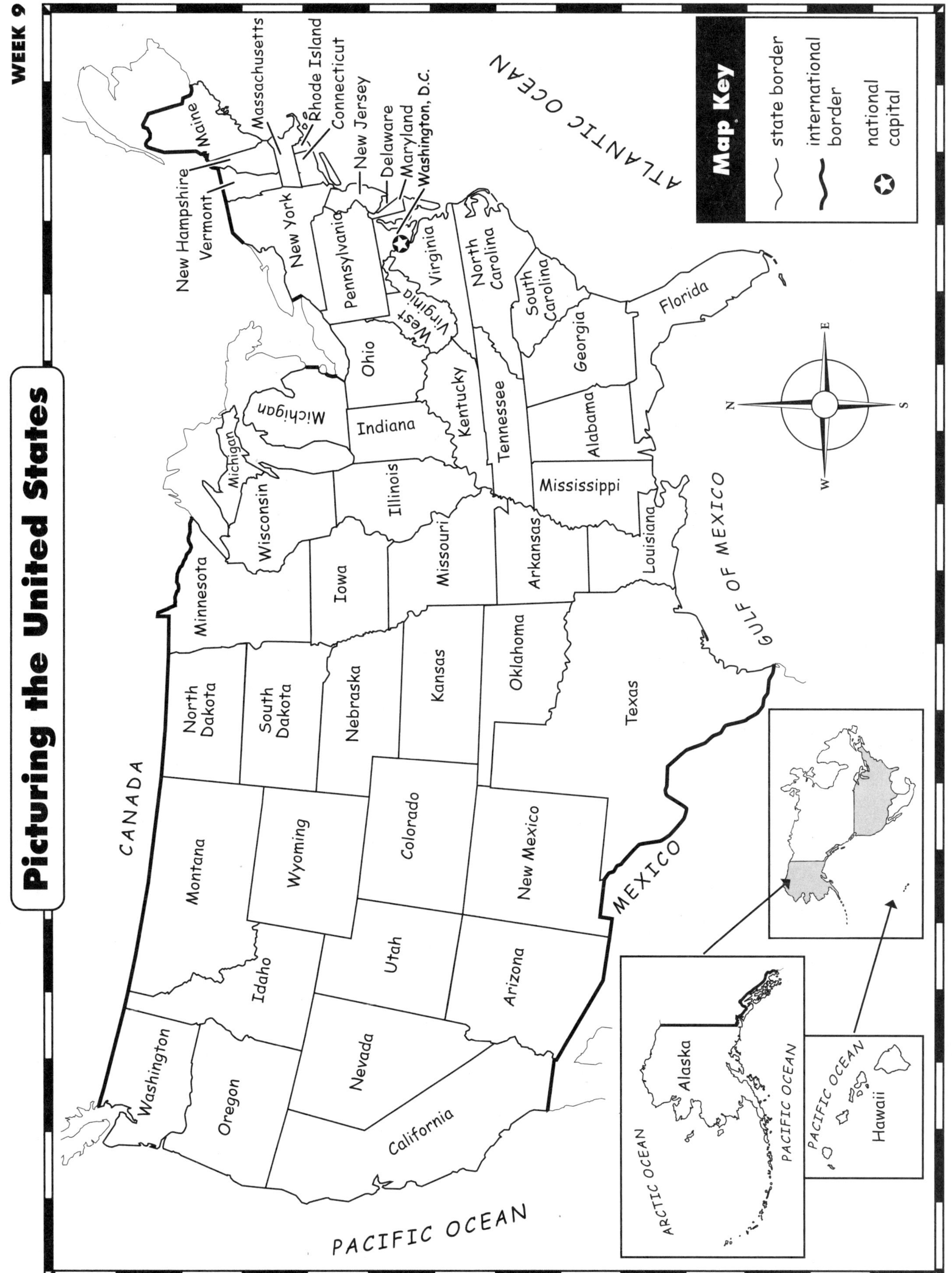

A Physical Map: Massachusetts

Massachusetts has a rugged coastline. Ships anchor in the safe harbors along the bays.

Massachusetts

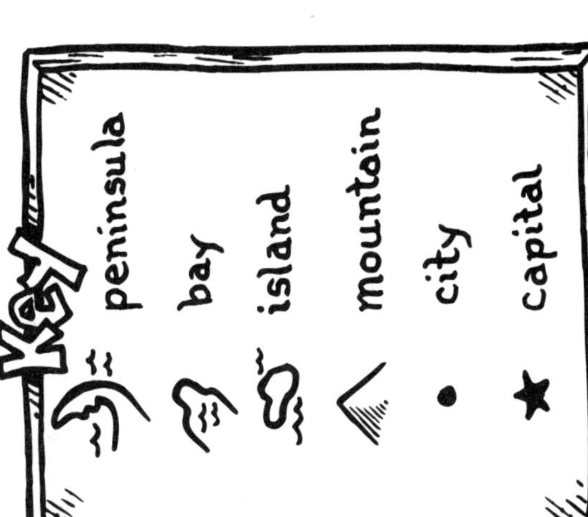

Key
- peninsula
- bay
- island
- mountain
- city
- capital

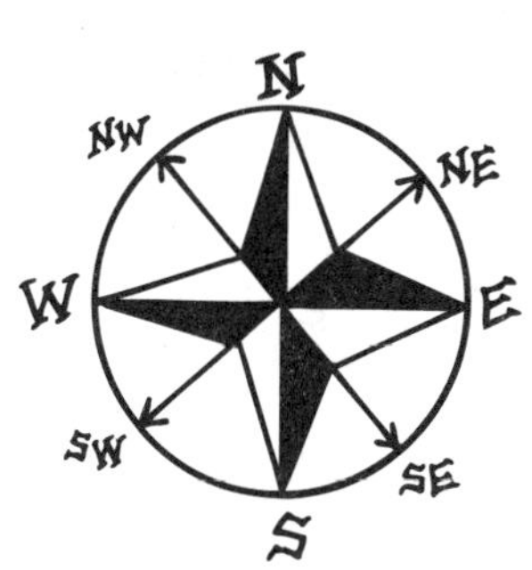

Living in a Community

Green Avenue

First Street

Brown Avenue

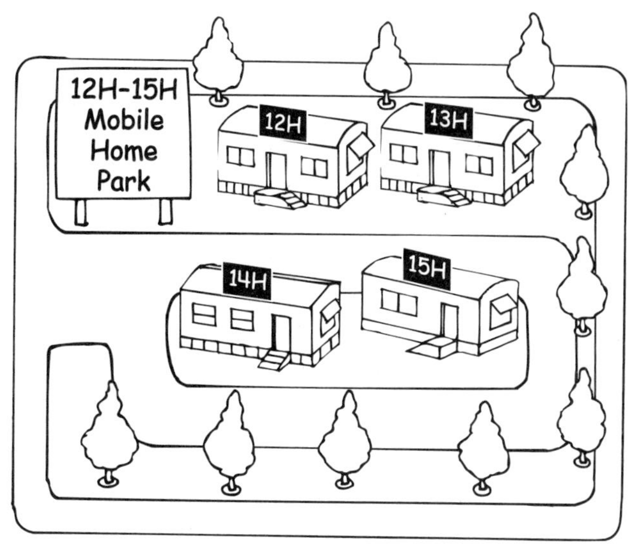

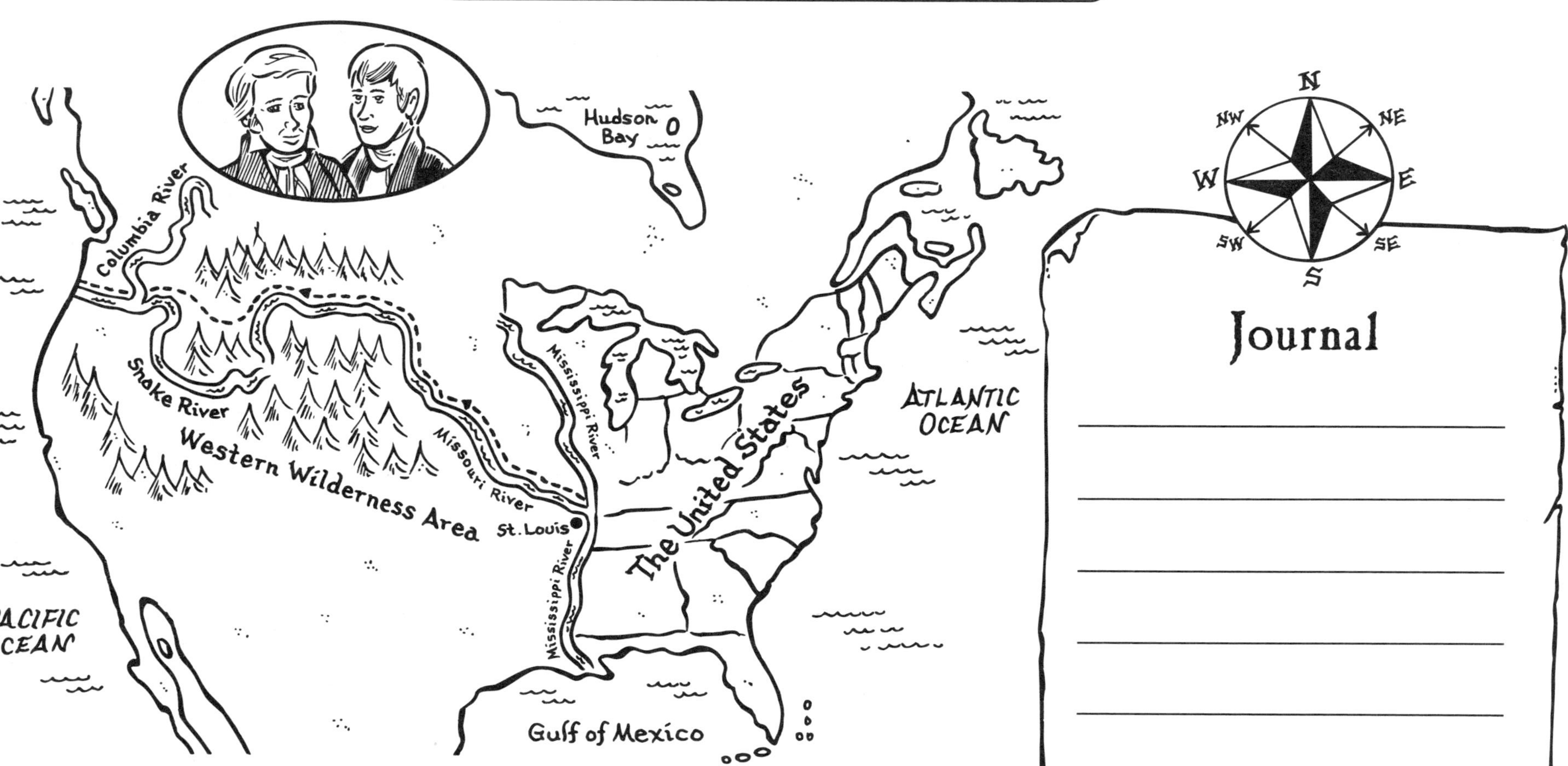

Transportation Routes in a Town

Thursday

1. In which direction do the train tracks run?

   ____

2. Which streets cross the train tracks?

   ____

Friday

1. Which street do you cross to get from the school to the park?

   ____

2. Which route runs alongside the railroad tracks?

   ____

Challenge

Use a blue marker to highlight the bike path on the map.

Daily Geography Practice • EMC 6853 • © Evan-Moor Corporation

The Pacific Region of the United States

Thursday

1. Which states border Canada?

____

2. Which state borders Mexico? _________________________

Friday

1. Which state is the largest in land area? Which two oceans border the state?

____

2. Which state is farthest north? Which state is farthest south?

____

Challenge

Part 1: Draw a line from the state to its capital. The first one has been completed for you. Use a United States map to help you.

State	Capital
Alaska	Salem
California	Olympia
Hawaii	Sacramento
Oregon	Juneau
Washington	Honolulu

Part 2: On the map, write the name of each capital next to the star on each state.

Daily Geography Practice • EMC 6853 • © Evan-Moor Corporation

A Weather Map

Daily Geography

Monday

1. How many states are shown on the map?

____

2. In which region of the United States are the states located?

____

Tuesday

1. What is the weather like in Kansas?

____

2. What is the weather like in Nebraska?

____

Wednesday

1. What is the weather like in Wisconsin and Michigan?

____

2. In which state is it snowing?

____

Oregon's Forests

Thursday

1. What is the state tree of Oregon?

   ____

2. How many national forests are in Oregon?

   ____

Friday

1. Eugene, Portland, and Salem are all on which river? What landforms are near the three cities?

   ____

   ____

2. Which states border Oregon? Do you think those states have forests?

   ____

Challenge

On the map, color the forests green. Choose an animal from the list and draw it on the map.

   Daily Geography Practice • EMC 6853 • © Evan-Moor Corporation

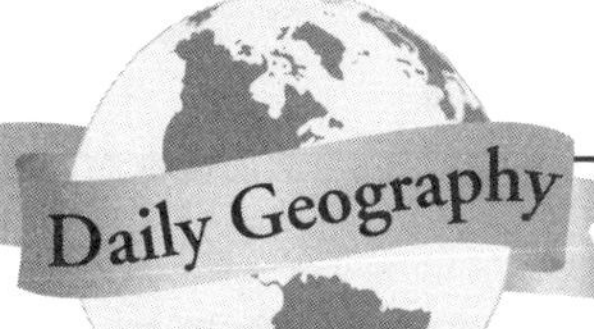

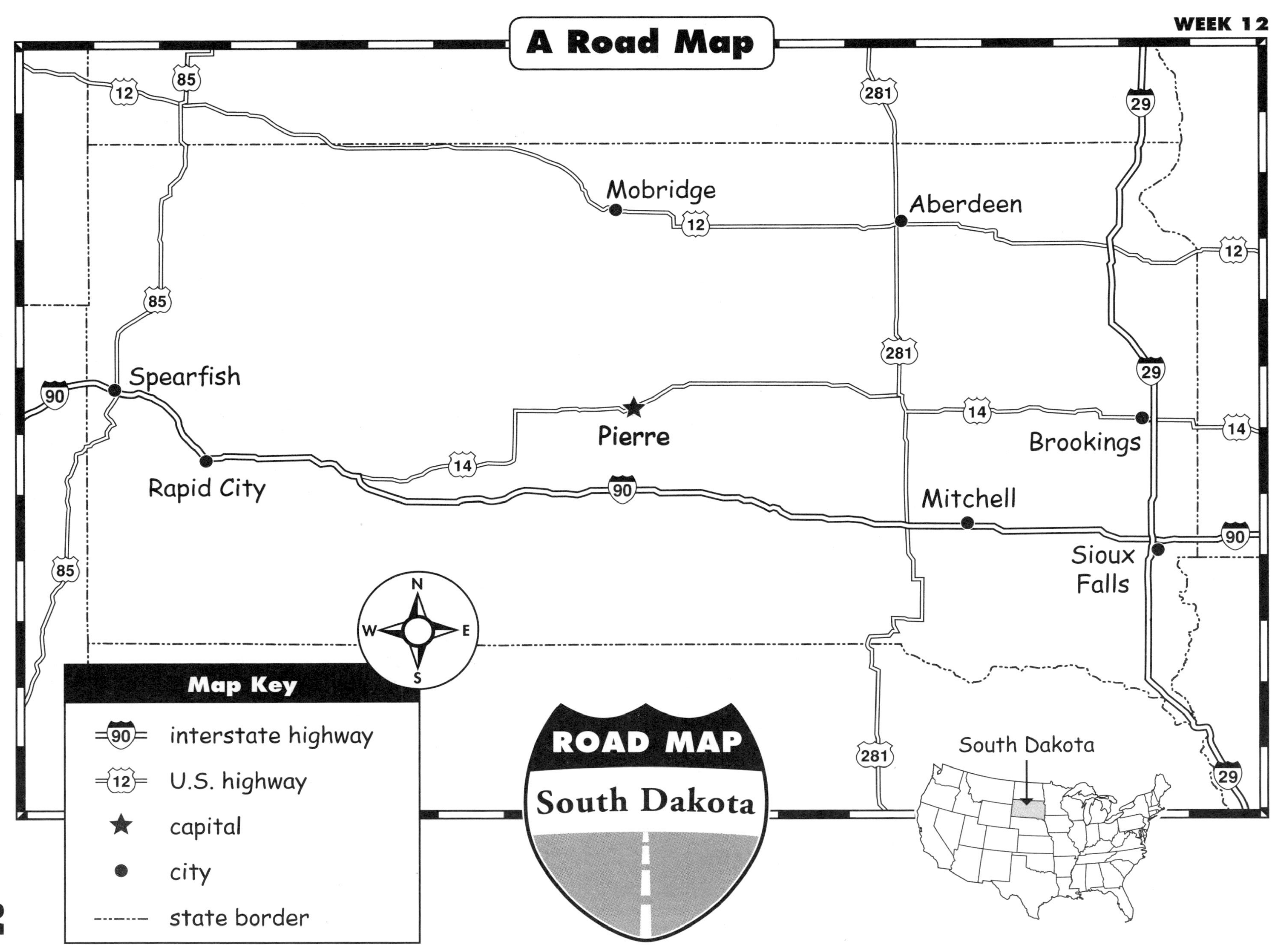
A Road Map
12
85
281
29
Mobridge
12
Aberdeen
12
85
281
29
Spearfish
90
14
Pierre
Brookings
14
Rapid City
14
90
Mitchell
85
90
Sioux Falls
N
W   E
S
Map Key
90   interstate highway
12   U.S. highway
capital
city
state border
ROAD MAP
South Dakota
281
South Dakota
29

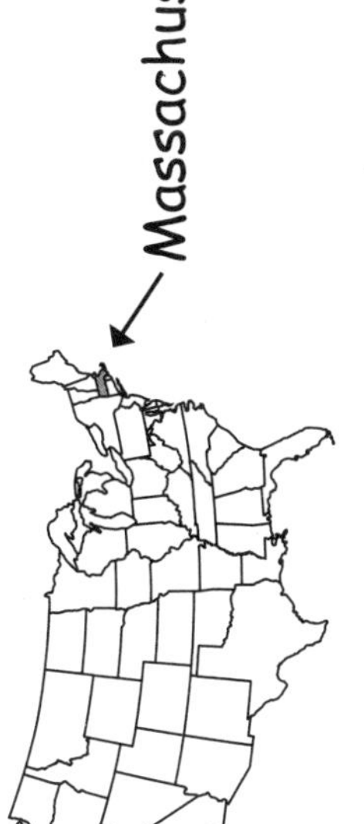

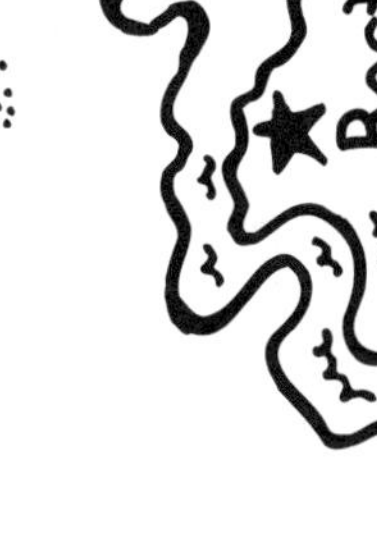
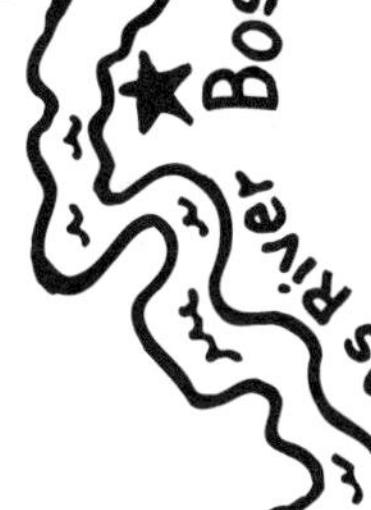
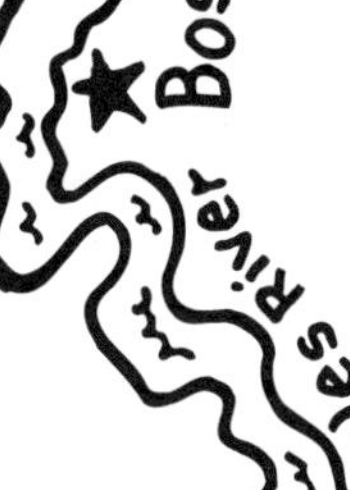
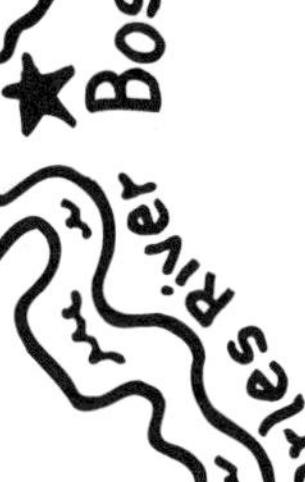
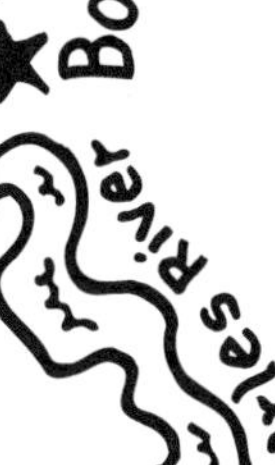
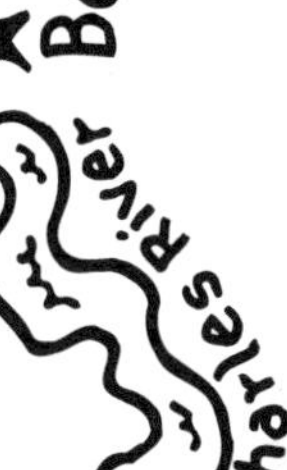

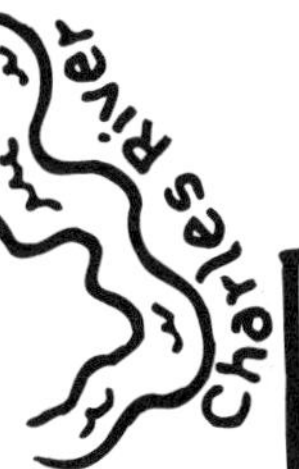
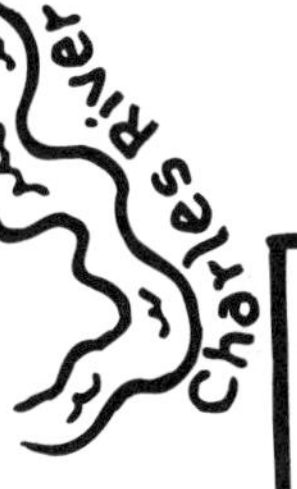

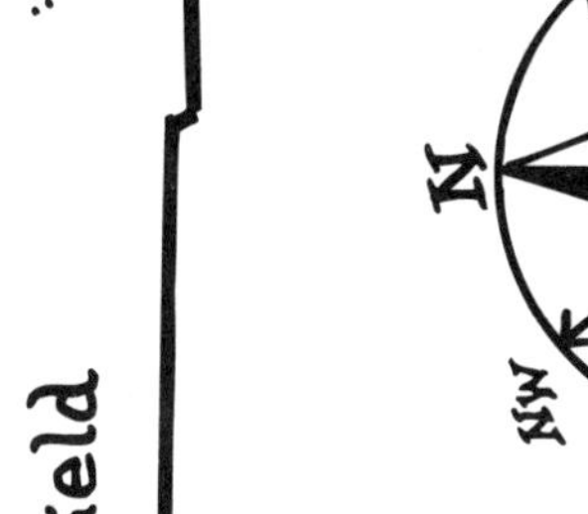

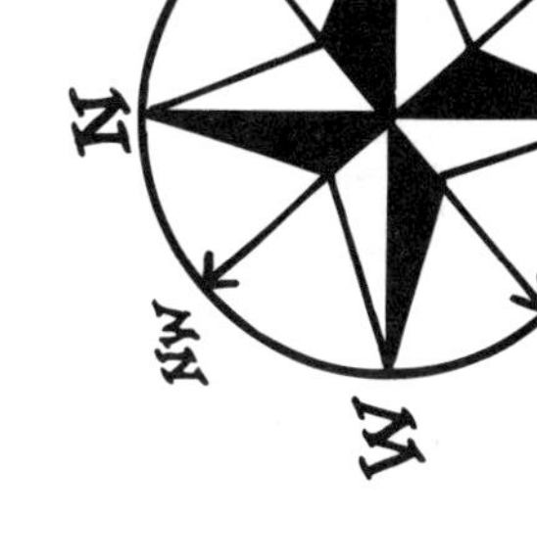

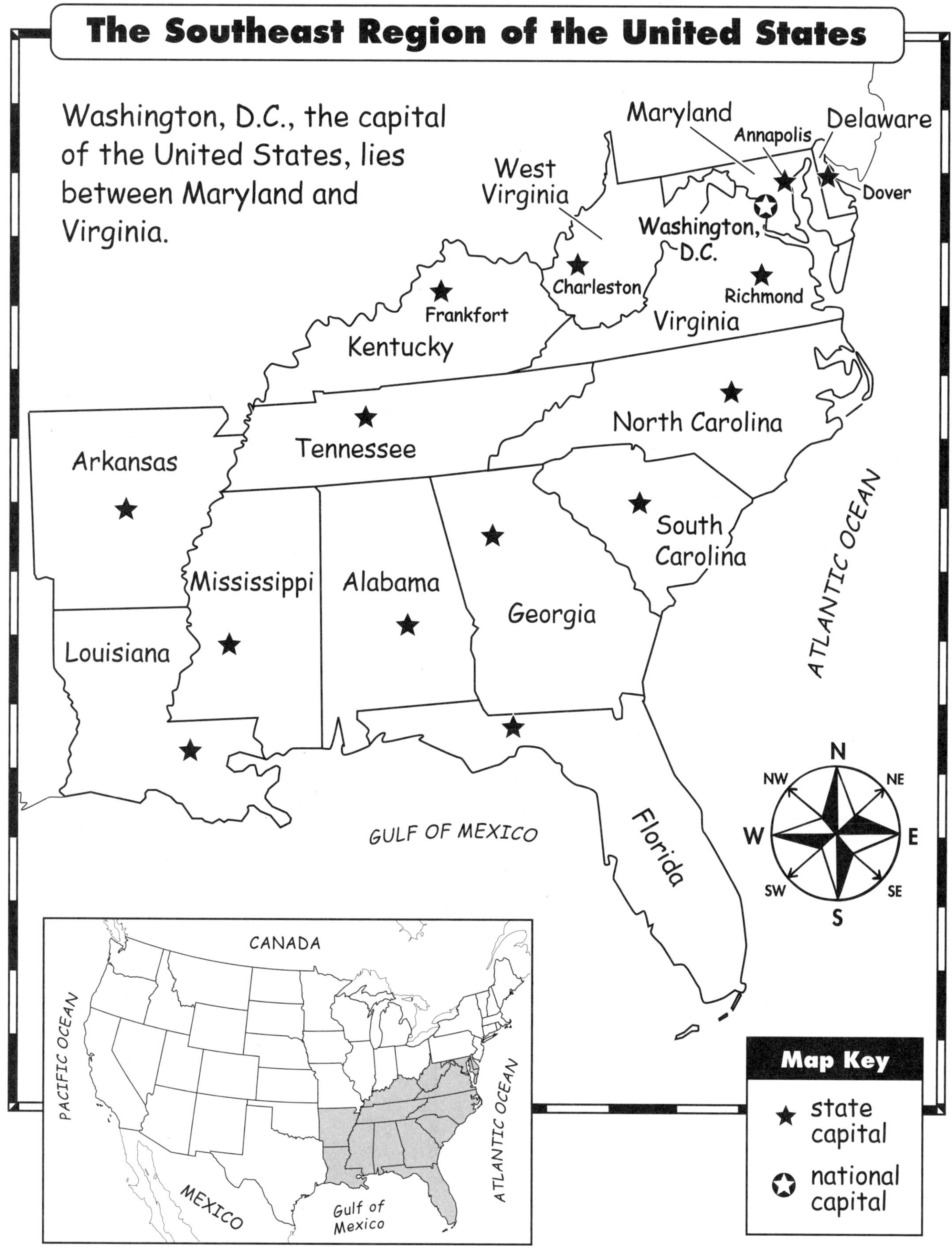

The Southeast Region of the United States
Washington, D.C., the capital of the United States, lies between Maryland and Virginia.
Maryland
Annapolis
Delaware
Dover
West Virginia
Washington, D.C.
Charleston
Frankfort
Kentucky
Richmond
Virginia
Tennessee
North Carolina
Arkansas
South Carolina
Mississippi
Alabama
Georgia
Louisiana
Florida
GULF OF MEXICO
ATLANTIC OCEAN
N
NW
NE
W
E
SW
SE
S
CANADA
PACIFIC OCEAN
ATLANTIC OCEAN
MEXICO
Gulf of Mexico
Map Key
state capital
national capital

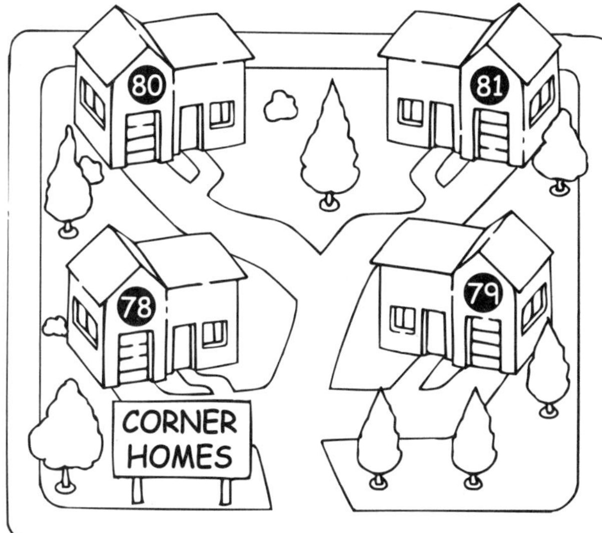

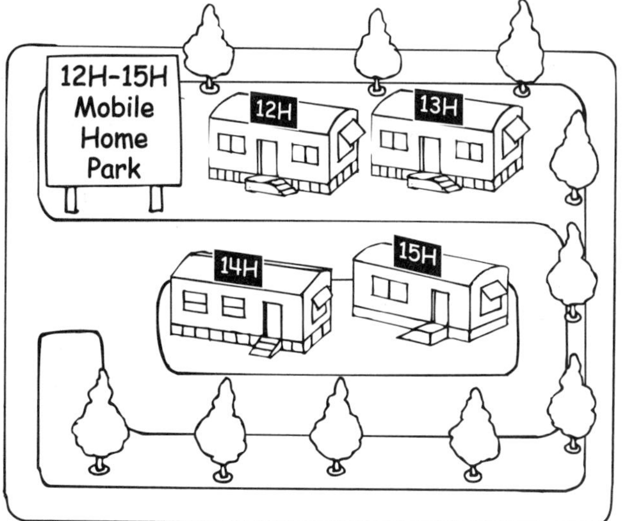

Intermediate Directions

Thursday

1. Which building is northwest of the post office?

   ____

2. Does First Avenue run east and west or north and south?

   ____

Friday

1. Start at the west end of Main Street. In which direction is the fountain?

   ____

2. What is found where Main Street and First Avenue cross?

   ____

Challenge

On the map, draw a book in the southeast corner of the library.

Draw a flagpole in the southwest corner of the school.

   Daily Geography Practice • EMC 6853 • © Evan-Moor Corporation

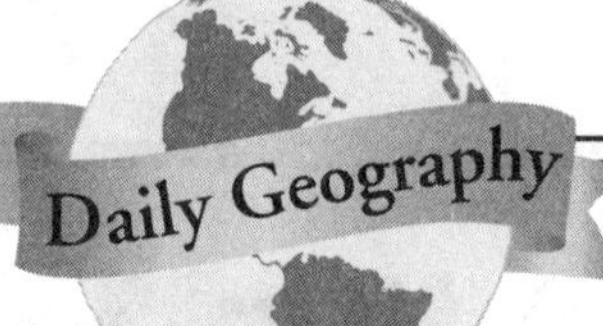

Picturing North America

Thursday

1. How many oceans border North America? Name them.

   ____

   ____

2. Name the two countries that border southern Mexico.

   ____

Friday

1. Name the largest island country east of Mexico.

   ____

2. Name the continent that is south of North America.

   ____

Challenge

On the map, trace the outline shape of North America in dark red. Place a blank piece of paper over the map. Trace over the lines that show through onto the blank piece of paper. Look at your drawing of North America. Close your eyes and make a mental picture of the shape of North America.

   Daily Geography Practice • EMC 6853 • © Evan-Moor Corporation

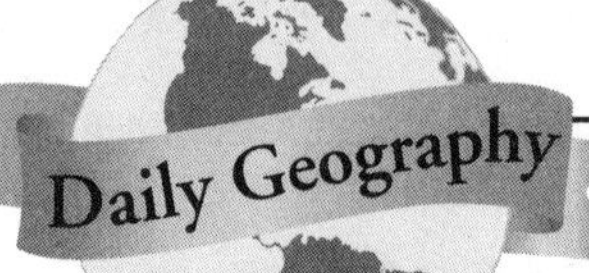

A Physical Map: Arizona

Thursday

1. In which part of the state is the Grand Canyon located?

   ____

2. Which river lies at the base of the Grand Canyon?

   ____

Friday

1. What is Arizona's nickname?

   ____

2. Name a state or country that borders Arizona.

   ____

Challenge

The Grand Canyon and the Painted Desert are very colorful. Color
the Grand Canyon and the Painted Desert in shades of yellow,
brown, red, and pink.

Daily Geography Practice • EMC 6853 • © Evan-Moor Corporation

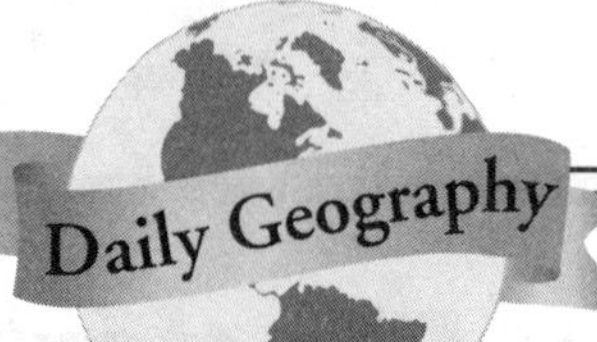

The Southeast Region of the United States

Thursday

1. Which four states do <u>not</u> border any labeled waterway?

   ____

2. How many states share a border with Alabama? _______________

Friday

1. Which state is a large peninsula with small islands off its coast?

   ____

2. Which two states are located in the northeast tip of the Southeast region?

   ____

Challenge

Five state capitals are labeled on the map of the Southeast region. Nine are not labeled. Write the names of the nine capitals on the correct states. Use a United States map to help you with the names.

Capitals

Baton Rouge	Little Rock	Raleigh
Columbia	Montgomery	Atlanta
Jackson	Nashville	Tallahassee

Daily Geography Practice • EMC 6853 • © Evan-Moor Corporation

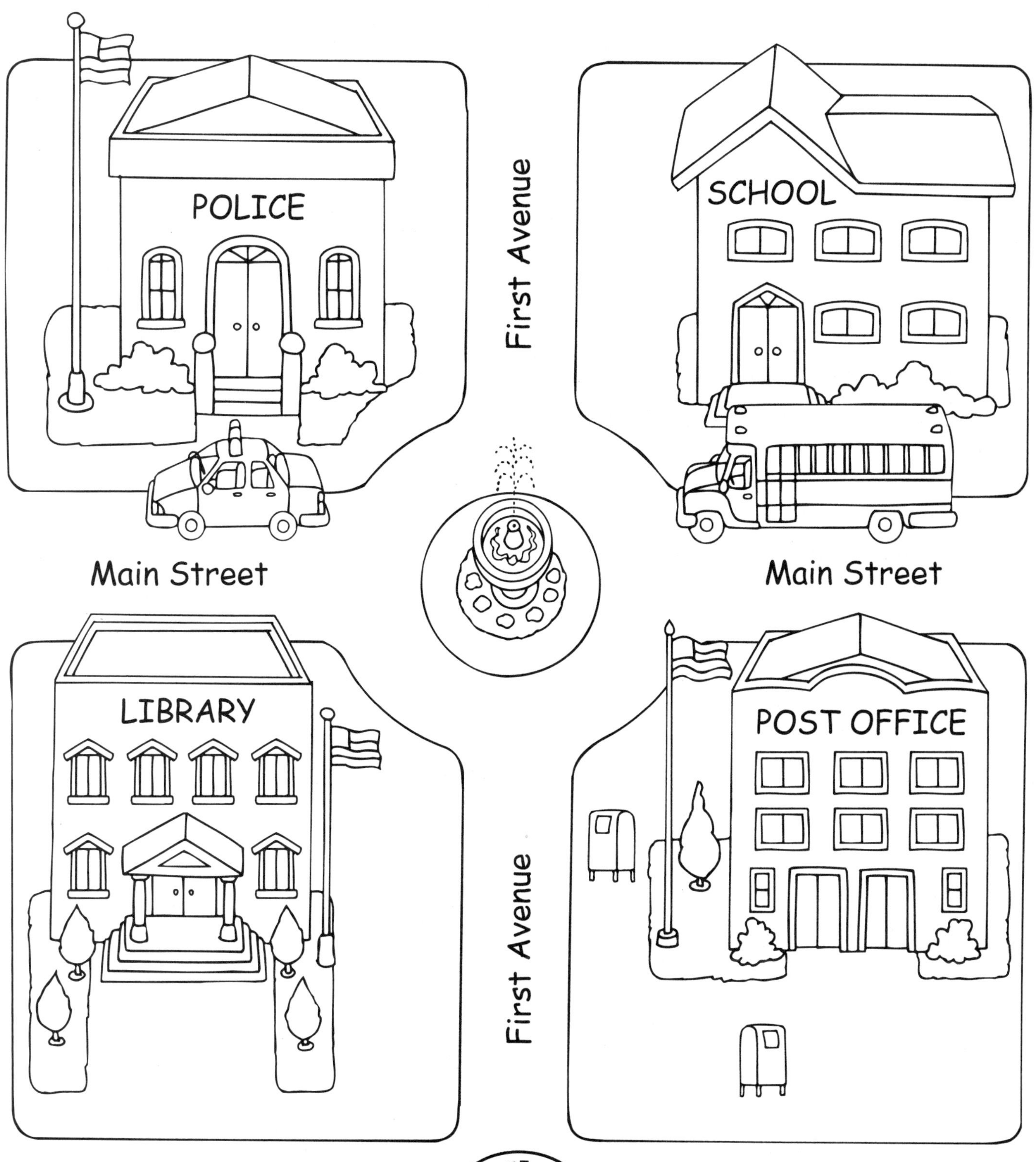

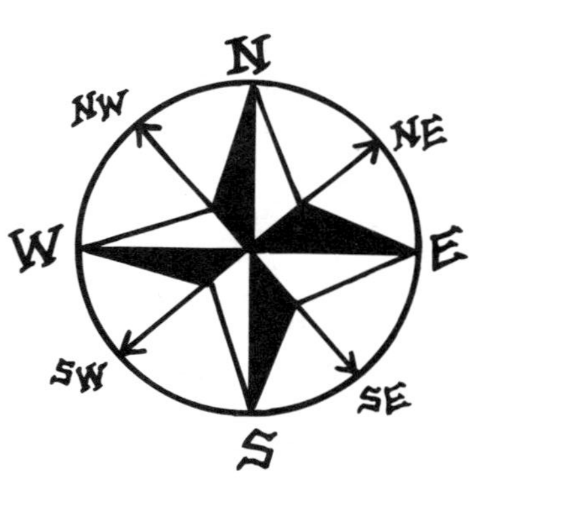
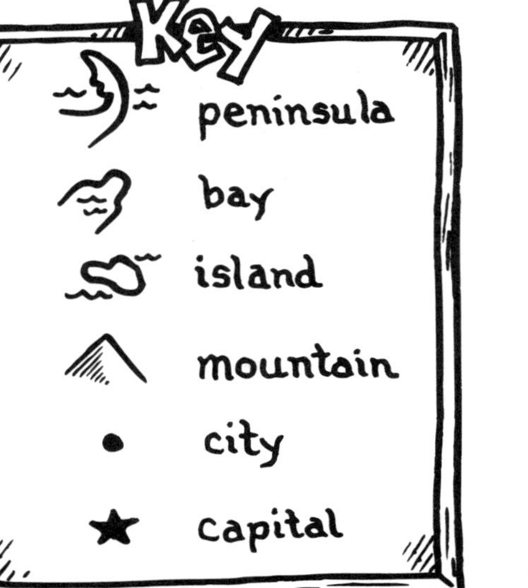
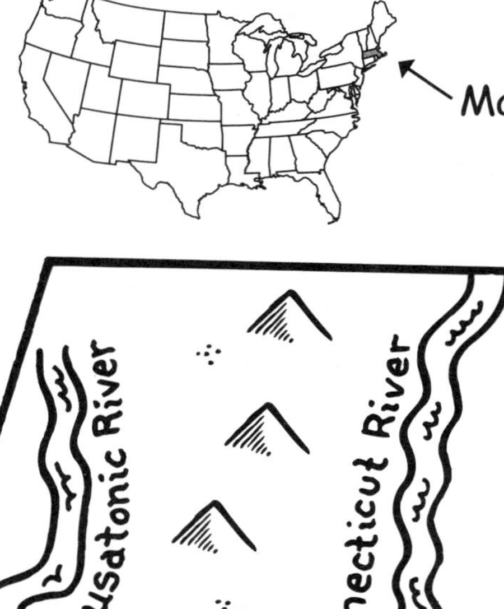
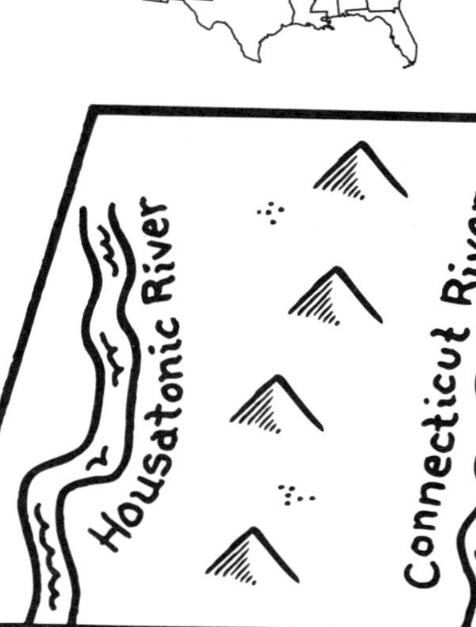
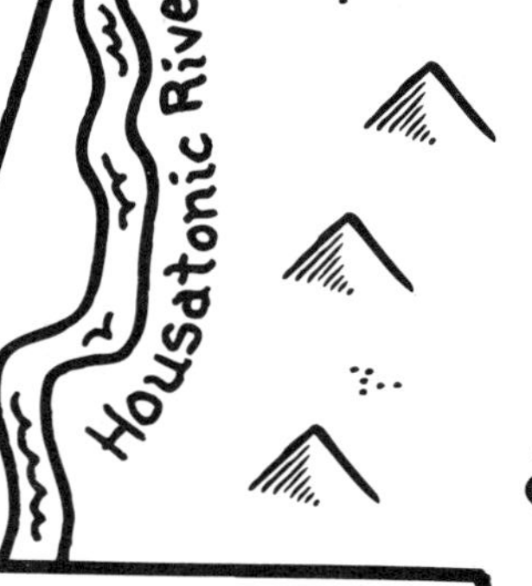
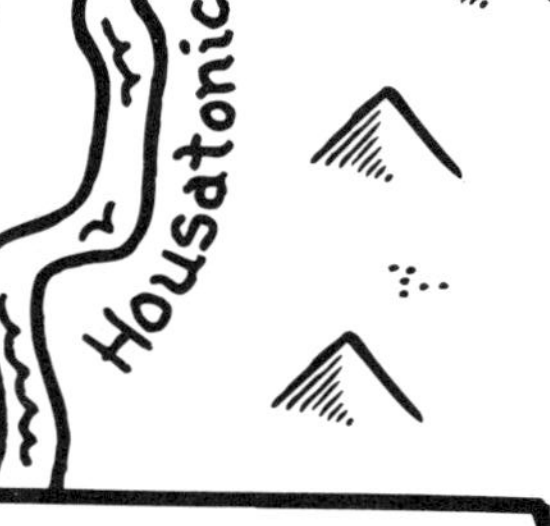

The Lewis and Clark Trail

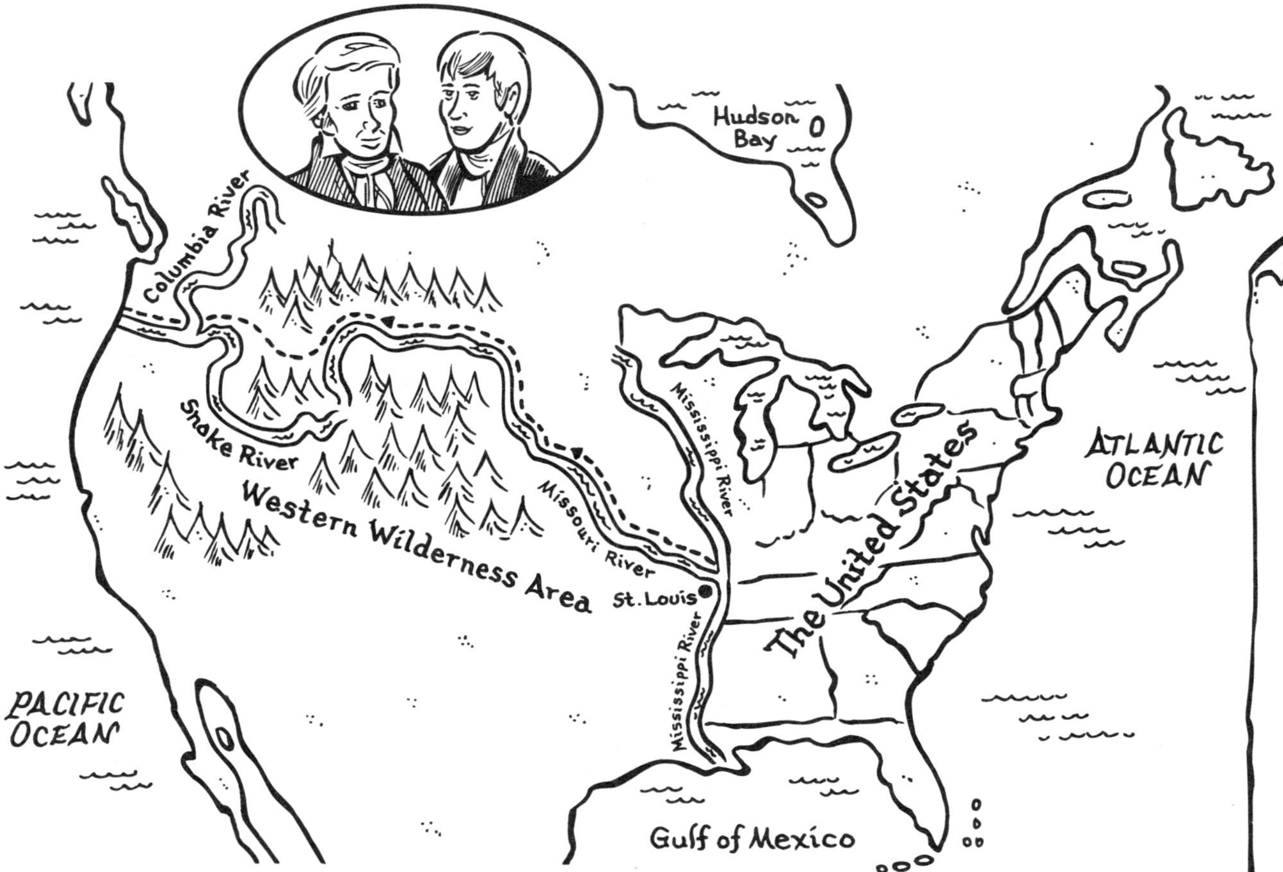

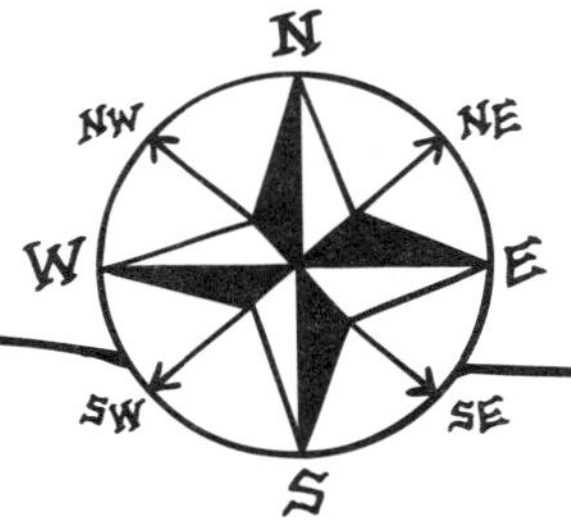

Journal

____

____

____

____

____

____

____

____

____

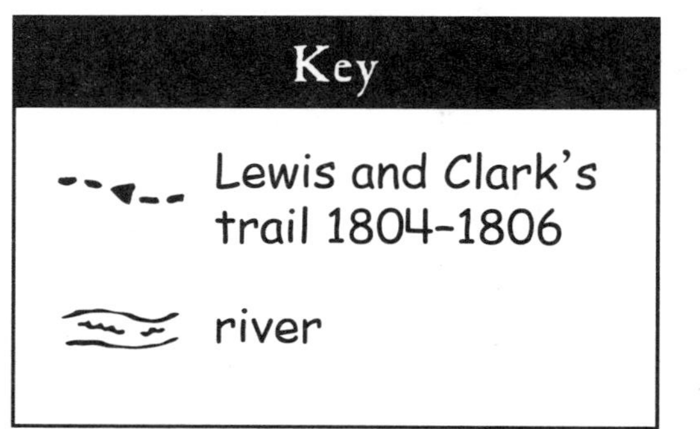

Key

- Lewis and Clark's trail 1804–1806
- river

Lewis and Clark were explorers. They traveled 8,000 miles (12,800 km) across the western wilderness. They discovered new lands for the United States.

A Road Map: South Dakota

Thursday

1. Which interstate highway runs through the city of Mitchell?

____

2. Name the cities along Interstate 29.

____

Friday

1. Which U.S. highways intersect in the city of Aberdeen?

____

2. Which interstate highway joins U.S. Highway 14?

____

Challenge

- Highlight the routes of the interstate highways in yellow.
- Highlight the routes of the U.S. highways in orange.

Daily Geography Practice • EMC 6853 • © Evan-Moor Corporation

The White House

Thursday

1. Where would a tourist see different kinds of fish? In which square is that building?

   ____

2. Where would a tourist see displays of America's past? In which square is that building?

   ____

Friday

1. How is George Washington, the first president, honored in the nation's capital?

   ____

   ____

2. Which cultural landmark is located in square C1?

   ____

Challenge

In square B1 on the map, draw your favorite symbol of America. Remember, it should be found in Washington, D.C.

 Daily Geography Practice • EMC 6853 • © Evan-Moor Corporation

A Weather Map

Thursday

1. Which state is 40° and partly cloudy? Which state is south of this state?

   ____

2. Which two states have temperatures of 60° and rain?

   ____

Friday

1. How many states border the Great Lakes?

   ____

2. Which state has the lowest temperature? Which state has the highest temperature?

   ____

Challenge

Choose which state in the North-Central region you would like
to visit. On the map page, write about the weather in that state.
Then write about the kinds of activities you could do in that kind of
weather.

     Daily Geography Practice • EMC 6853 • © Evan-Moor Corporation

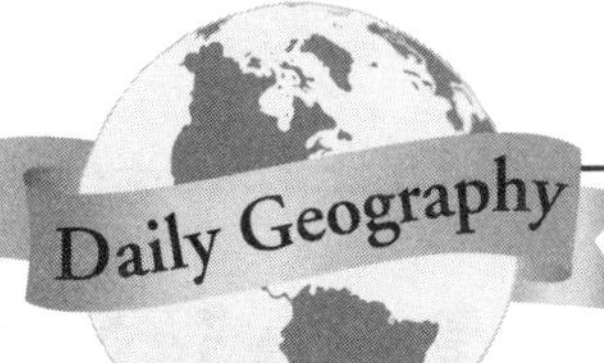

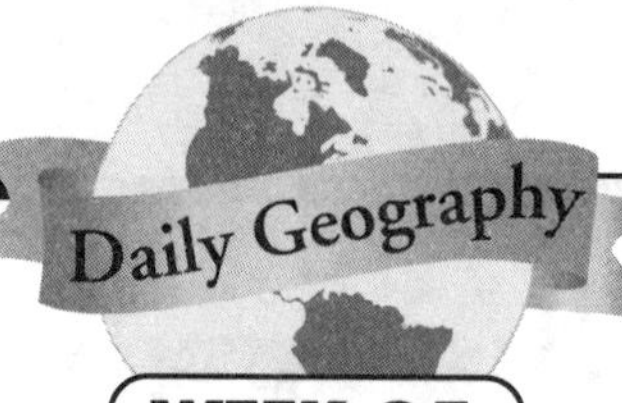

Parts of a Map

The parts of the map include a title, a map key, and a compass rose.

This is the title. The title tells the name of the map.

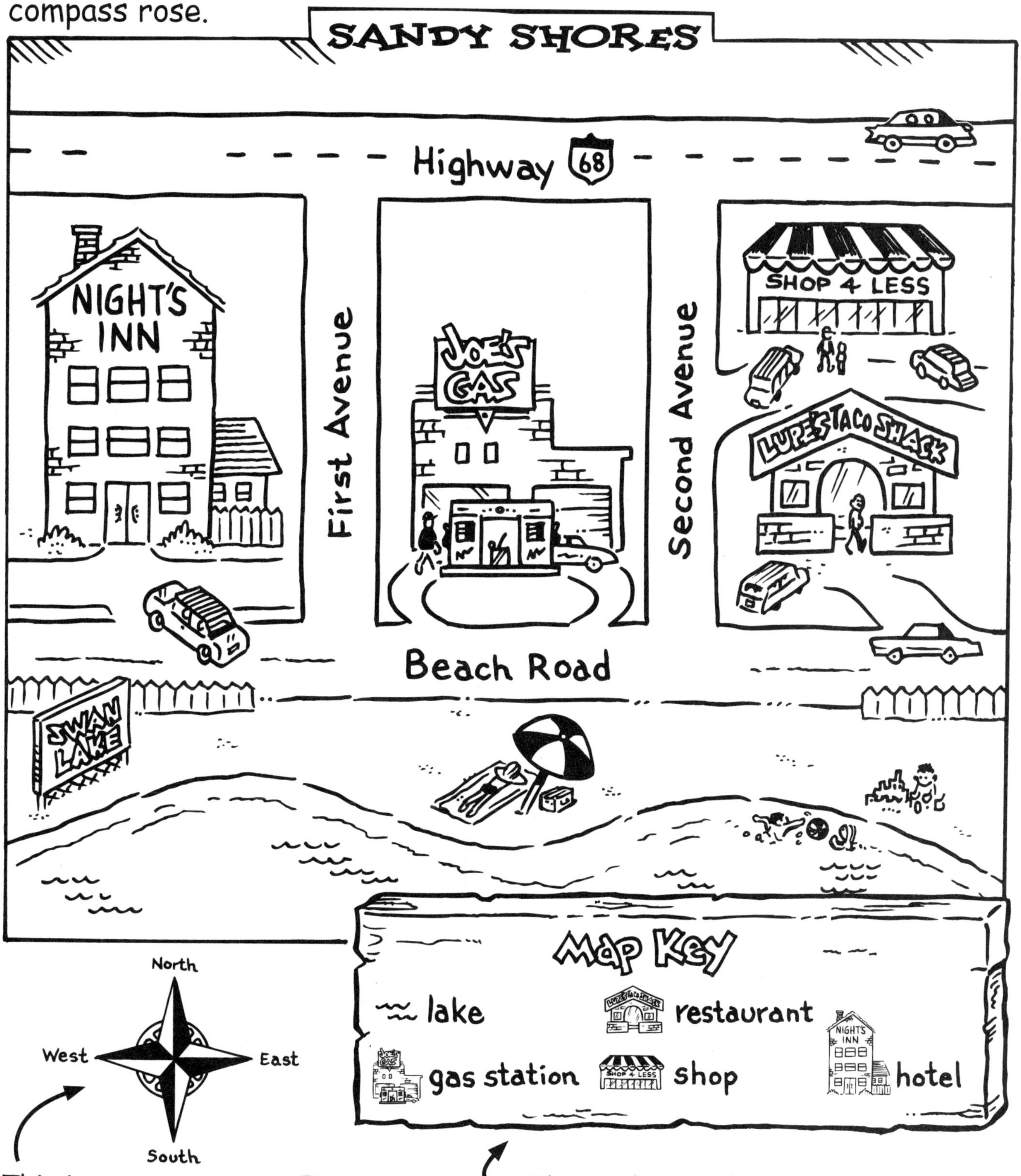

SANDY SHORES
Highway 68
NIGHT'S INN
First Avenue
JOE'S GAS
Second Avenue
SHOP 4 LESS
LUPE'S TACO SHACK
Beach Road
SWAN LAKE
North
West
East
South
Map Key
lake
restaurant
gas station
shop
hotel

This is a compass rose. It shows directions on a map.

This is the map key. It has symbols that stand for something on the map.

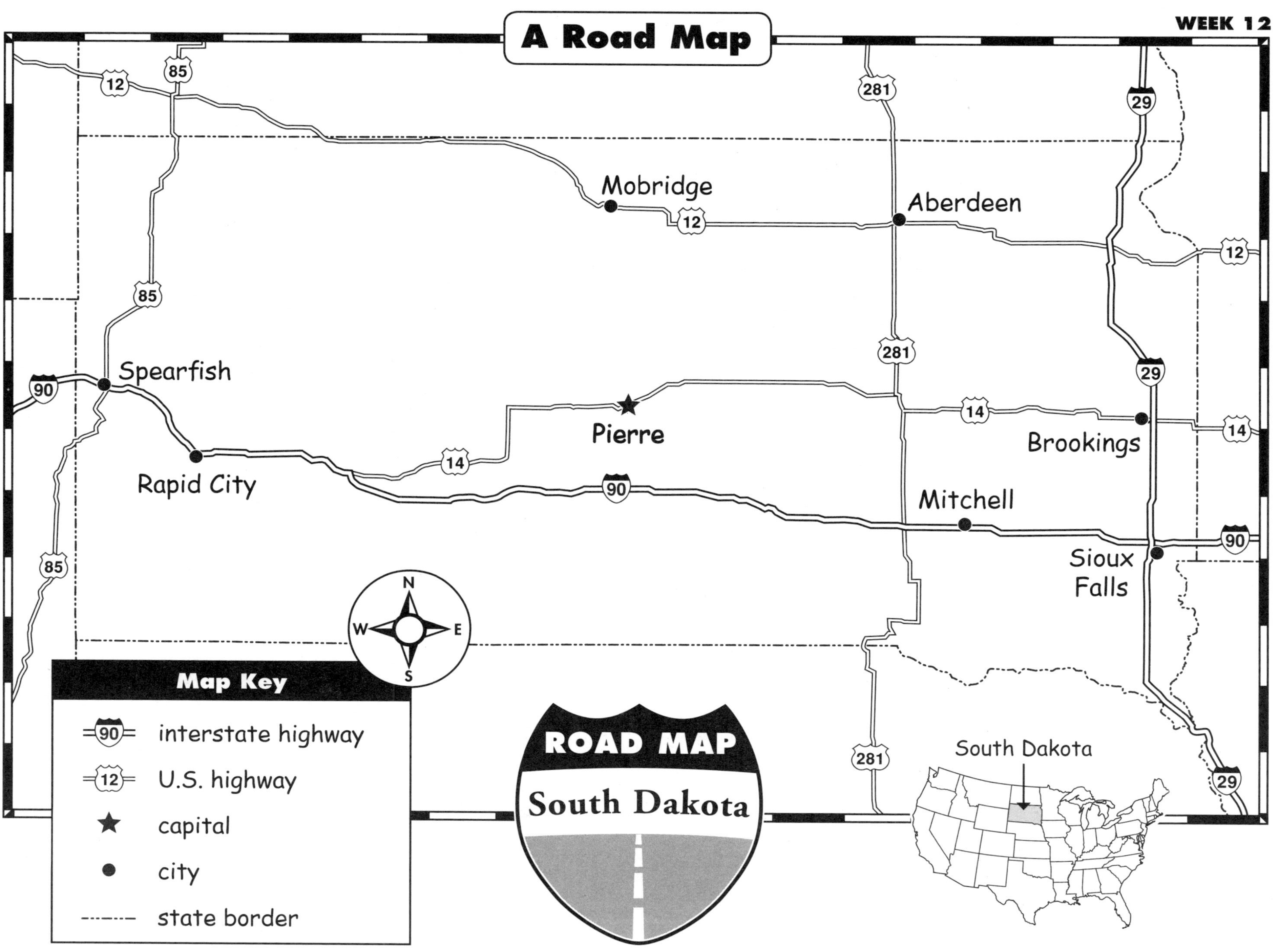

A Road Map
Mobridge
Aberdeen
Spearfish
Pierre
Rapid City
Brookings
Mitchell
Sioux Falls
12
85
281
29
12
281
29
85
14
14
14
90
90
85
281
29
N
E
S
W
Map Key
interstate highway
U.S. highway
capital
city
state border
90
12
ROAD MAP
South Dakota
South Dakota

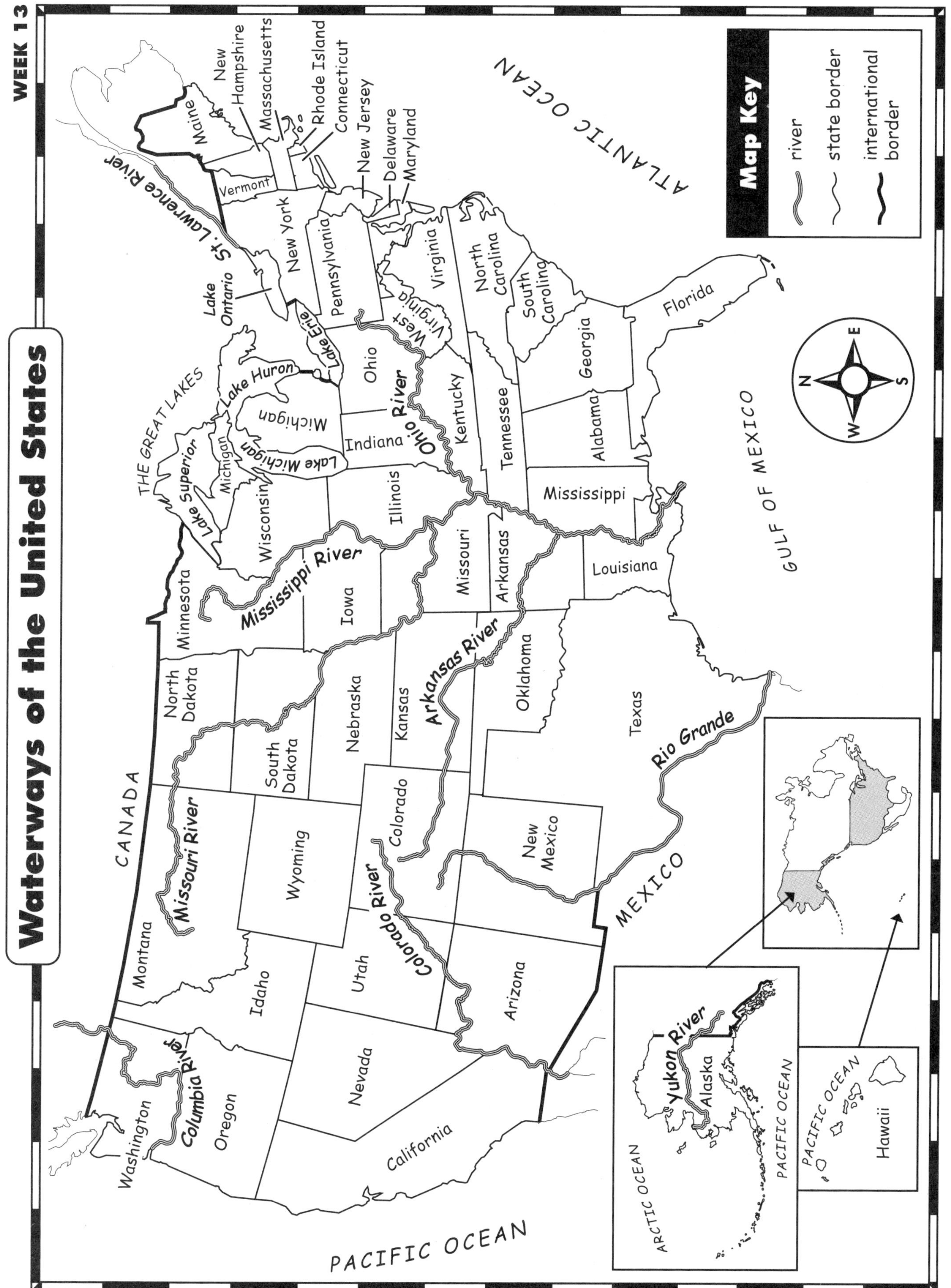

A Physical Map: Massachusetts

Massachusetts has a rugged coastline. Ships anchor in the safe harbors along the bays.

Massachusetts

Atlantic Ocean

Merrimack River

Massachusetts Bay

Provincetown

Cape Cod Bay

Cape Cod Peninsula

Nantucket Sound

Nantucket

Martha's Vineyard

Boston

Buzzards Bay

Charles River

Worcester

Springfield

Connecticut River

Housatonic River

Atlantic Ocean

NW N NE
W E
SW S SE

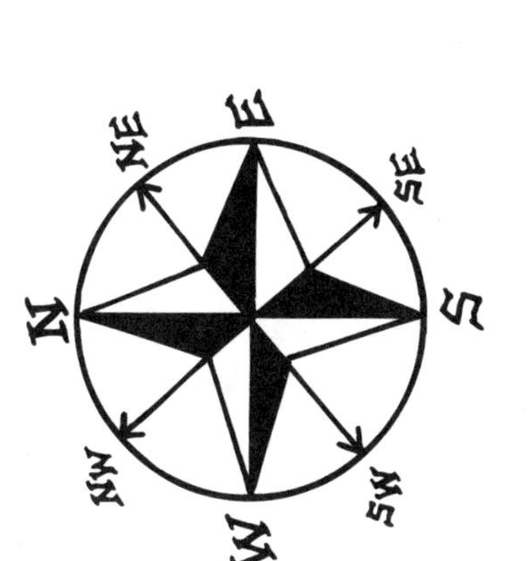

The Pacific Region of the United States

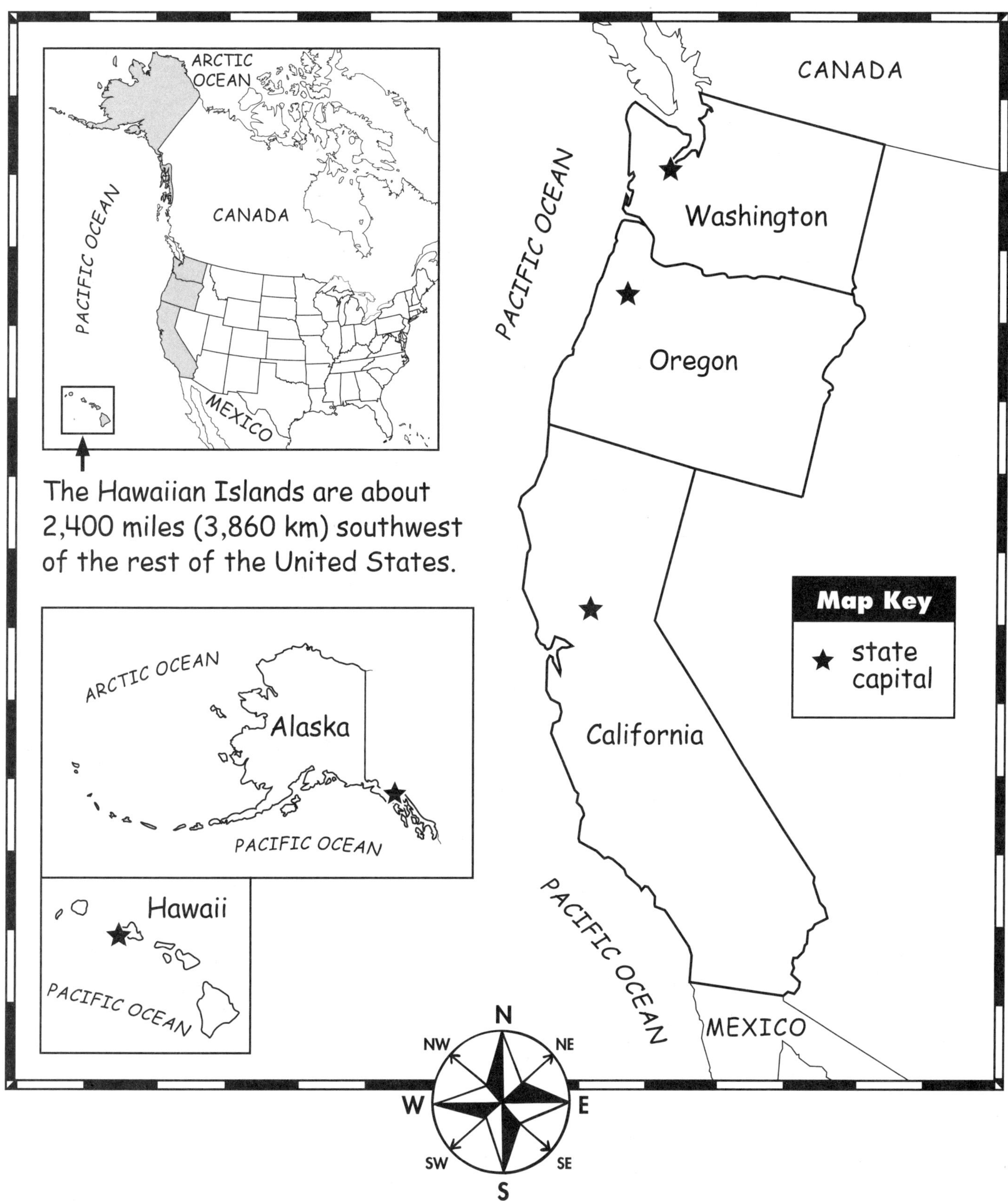

The Hawaiian Islands are about 2,400 miles (3,860 km) southwest of the rest of the United States.

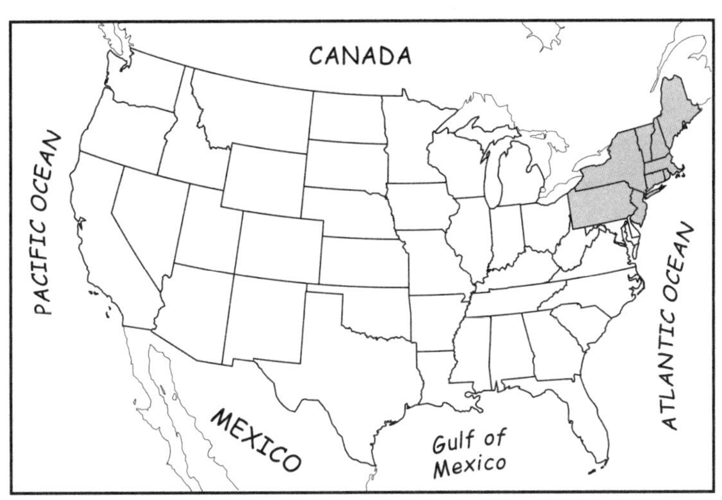

A Tourist Map

California

People who travel for fun are called tourists.

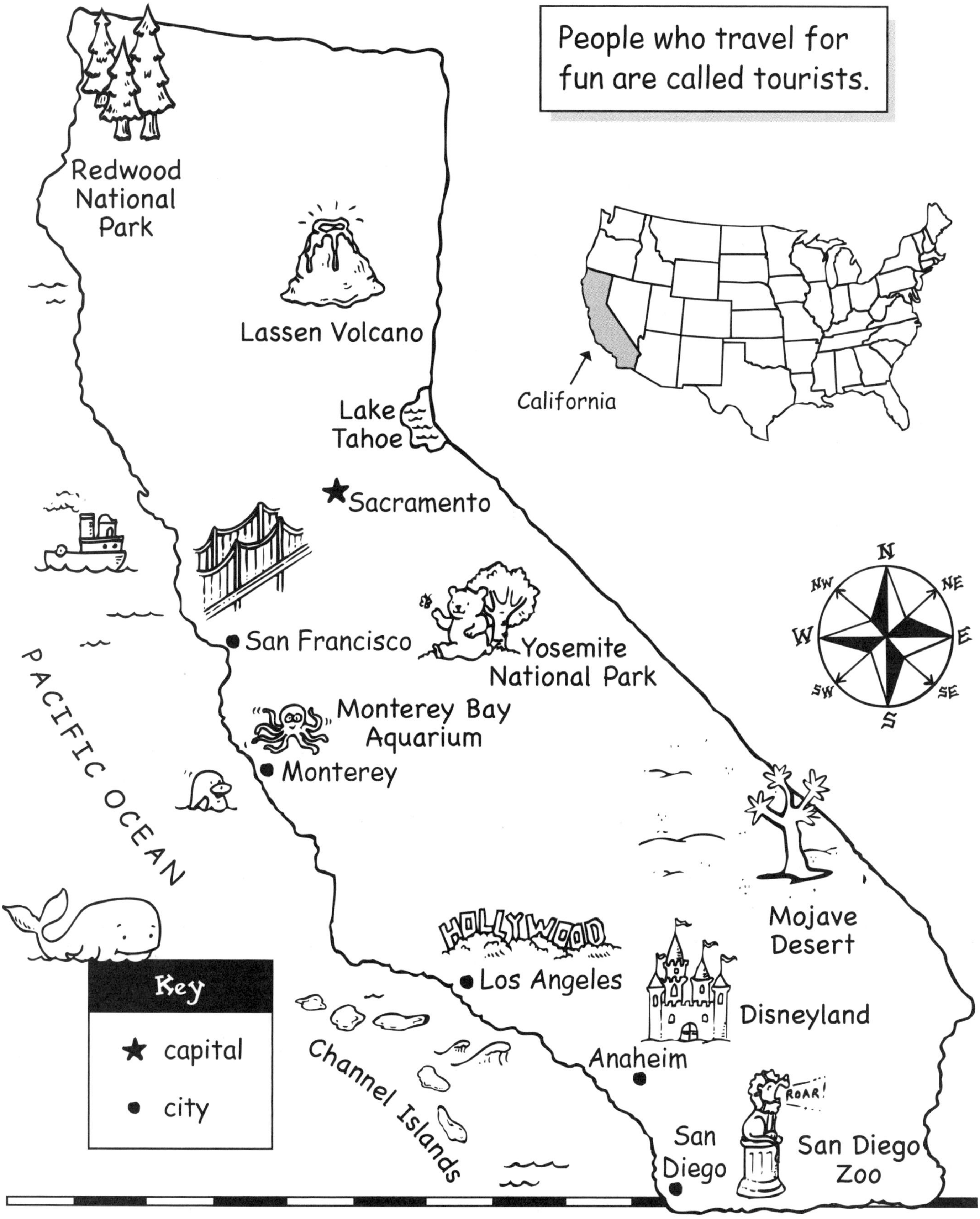